Flashpacking throu

Travels through 17 African Nations

By Jason Smart

Published by Smart Travel Publishing

Text and Photographs © 2013 Jason Smart

All Right Reserved. No part of this book may be reproduced or transmitted in any form or by any means, electronic or mechanical, including photocopying, recording, or any information storage and retrieval system, without prior written permission of the Author.

For my wife, who enjoyed Africa as much as I did

CONTENTS

Chapter 1: Charmless Charmers and Unsavoury Guides — 1

Chapter 2: Bumster Madness in West Africa — 15

Chapter 3: A Day Trip to Senegal — 33

Chapter 4: Johannesburg to Swaziland — 43

Chapter 5: A Daytrip to the KIngdom in the Sky — 53

Chapter 6: The Cape — 61

Chapter 7: Paradise in the Indian Ocean — 69

Chapter 8: Land of the Pharaohs — 81

Chapter 9: Onwards to Addis Ababa — 95

Chapter 10: Spice Island — 107

Chapter 11: Livingstone — 117

Chapter 12: Chasing Warthogs in Zimbabwe — 125

Chapter 13: Dancing with the Hippos from Hell! — 131

Chapter 14: Going Solo in Uganda — 141

Chapter 15: Remembering the Past in Rwanda — 155

Chapter 16: Motorbikes and Prostitutes — 167

Chapter 17: Where is the Comoros? — 179

Chapter 18: The Final Stop – Dar es Salaam — 191

Afterword — 199

Chapter 1: Charmless Charmers and Unsavoury Guides

Interesting fact: The Shrine of Sidi Yahya, in Eastern Morocco, reportedly contains the tomb of John the Baptist.

"Hello!" said the man in the long blue robe and charcoal headcovering. His black beard and dark features added stark contrast to his royal blue neck scarf. He looked about thirty years of age.

Angela and I were walking towards Marrakech's old town. We'd just visited Majorelle Gardens, owned by none other than Yves Saint Laurent, and we wanted to get to the central square for a coffee, before hitting the souqs.

"I am not guide," the man said in broken English as he walked alongside us. "I only wish to practise English with nice people. Perhaps I talk with you?"

For most of the day, Angela and I had been hassled by people left, right and centre. They were trying to either sell us something, or guide us somewhere we didn't want to go. *'I take you to tanneries!'* was a common opening gambit, referring to the place where animal hides were prepared in Marrakech. Another was, *'You want hashish? I get you good hashish!'* But this was always directed at me. The snake charmers in Djemaa el Fna, the central square, had already ripped us off too. After draping snakes upon our heads and shoulders, then taking a few photos (with our camera), the charmless charmers had demanded money.

"Four hundred dirham!" one of the men had said with a toothless grin. All around us was a cacophony of musical instruments and banging of drums, as well as the clickety-clack of carts being pushed towards the souqs. A man with two monkeys waited nearby, trying to entice another couple into posing with them.

I looked at the snake charmer and shook my head. Four hundred dirham was about thirty pounds. "No way."

Both men looked offended. "Yes! We take many photo!" one of them said. "Four hundred dirham is price. You pay right now!"

After a few minutes of haggling, we relented and gave them two hundred. We would have given even less had we possessed smaller notes. If only we'd visited one of the orange juice stalls that lined the square to get some change first. Lesson one learnt: carry small value notes in Morocco. And with the man in blue trailing after us, we were about to learn lesson number two...

2

"My name is Muhammad, and I am Berber," he said. "You must be heading for square. I take you there as gift."

Berbers were the indigenous people of North Africa. They had lived on the edge of the Sahara for centuries. Historically, Berber tribes had been farmers and nomads, but in modern times, many had moved into the cities. Muhammad was one of them.

Angela and I said nothing. Doing so would only bring about more talk of tanneries or perhaps of a cousin's lamp shop. We carried on walking, hoping he'd take the hint. Ahead of us, a large woman in a headscarf mounted a motorbike and then, with a blast of power, she was off.

Unofficial guides were a problem in Marrakech. In fact, they had become such a major irritant to tourists that the authorities had been forced to act. Undercover police patrolled the old town as well as key places of interest, searching out unofficial guides and removing them if found. But in other parts of town, like the one we were now in, men such as Muhammad had a free rein.

Crossing a road, we quickened our pace. Muhammad stopped on the other side shaking his head. "If heading to square," he shouted, "you go wrong way! Square this way! Please come! I show you!"

We ignored him. We hurried along a street full of metalwork and hardware shops. Some of the copper kettles outside one shop were enormous.

"Okay," said Muhammad after catching up with us. "We get to square this way. Take longer that is all."

3

Ahead of us were the salmon-pink walls of the old city, stretching for nineteen kilometres. Made of red clay and chalk, Marrakech's old town was called the *Red City,* and it wasn't hard to see why. Angela and I headed towards a busy gate cutting through the 30-foot walls, hoping it would lead us to the central square. Muhammad doggedly stuck to our side.

The gate was crowded with hawkers trying to sell sunglasses and cheap watches, but we passed them and entered the medina within. Narrow, stone alleyways with cobblestone floors cut their way through stone arches and clay buildings. A horse and cart stood just inside the entrance; its cargo of chickens creating a hullabaloo until we passed it. It was like stepping back in time.

"Many buildings were homes of rich men," Muhammad said jovially. "Wealthy men would own a few buildings, all close together. One would be for him and his wives, the others for his concubines." Muhammad looked at me, grinning. "Good life, eh!"

I had to admit that Muhammad seemed a knowledgeable fellow, and he certainly seemed friendly enough. Plus, it was interesting having him around to point things out that we would have ordinarily missed. How much was true, however, was anyone's guess.

"Come," he said. "I show you university. Is very beautiful building. You take many good photo. Then I take you to square."

I looked at Angela and shrugged. We followed our new guide through the rabbit warren of the northern medina, a labyrinth, every turn taking us deeper within. A few small stores sold grocery products, and above our heads, clothes dangled from wooden awnings. Suddenly a donkey clattered past, heavily laden with goods for the market, its owner sitting on the edge of his cart.

"This is old university," said Muhammad when we arrived at a small square. The three of us stopped to admire the buildings around the edge. Arches that looked like oversized keyholes and beautifully patterned walls made the small square a delightful sight. "It used to hold nine hundred students but was closed in 1960," explained Muhammad. "It is now a historical building."

After taking some photos we all moved off, with Muhammad now firmly in the lead.

4

The crowds thinned out. We followed the man in blue, wondering when we would get to the central square. We were in his hands now, and that was that. In a quiet alleyway, Muhammad sidled up to me. "You are not first people I help in Marrakech. And even though I not *official* guide, people often pay me for my time and kindness." He smiled. "Perhaps you will pay me later if you wish – but before that, let me tell you something of my people, the Berber."

Muhammad informed us that the Berber people were fine artisans but had a big problem in Marrakech. "The authorities will only allow four days in whole year when we can sell the goods we make. So you are lucky to be in Marrakech today! It is Berber selling day! Come, I show you!"

We didn't feel lucky. Muhammad probably wanted to show us his brother's fabric shop or his uncle's leather store. We came to a more populated part of the medina where people sat about in doorways drinking tea and smoking cigarettes. Some individuals even waved at Muhammad. Others simply stared at Angela. We didn't have a clue where we were.

After a short while, Muhammad stopped outside a dingy-looking shop. It looked like someone's house, except for a few carpets dangling outside the door.

"This is quality Berber carpet shop," said Muhammad. "I not make money for bringing you here – that I promise – I just want you to see fine quality of artisan. Come, come, follow please!"

I could tell that Angela had had enough of the charade. And I felt the same. We had no interest in carpets, Berber or otherwise.

"No," I said, standing our ground. "We just want to get to the square."

Muhammad smiled disarmingly. "Yes, but carpets are of finest quality. You do not have to buy. Just look. Please come! Only for one minute"

I shook my head. "No."

Muhammad paused for a moment, seemingly at a loss, but then quickly regained his composure. "As you wish. You do not like the carpet, I understand. I take you to square. Please come." We left the doorway and followed him down another alleyway.

5

Muhammad seemed less jovial than before. Perhaps he realised we were not going to visit any of his *brothers'* stores. In a deserted alleyway, he stopped and turned to face us. "I am good guide, yes?"

We stopped, and Angela nodded uncertainly.

He said, "Yes, and people pay me for being good guide. They always very generous. You pay me now!"

I shook my head. "You haven't taken us to the square, so why should we pay you?"

"Because I take time to show you old town."

I took Angela's hand, and we walked past him. We quickened our pace, hoping to come to a more populated part of the medina, perhaps even one we recognised. Muhammad caught up with us. This time he raised his voice. "You pay now!"

We ignored him until we arrived at another crossroad of alleyways. There were a few people in sight, and so we stopped to face our tormentor. For all I knew, he had a knife hidden in his robes somewhere.

"How much do you want?" I asked

"Four hundred dirham."

Four hundred dirham again, I realised. It seemed the standard rate for ripping off tourists in Marrakech.

"No way." I said, fishing about in my pocket for some small change. "You can have twenty and be done with it."

"*Twenty!* I cannot feed my family for that. You must give four hundred."

I shook my head and handed him a twenty note. "That's all you'll get. Take it or leave it."

Surprisingly, Muhammad accepted the note and pocketed it within a second. "Okay, square that way. Good-bye." And with that, he disappeared from sight.

Lesson number two had been a good one: trust no one in Marrakech.

6

In times gone by, the heads of executed people were placed on spikes in Marrakech's main square. This grisly fact was the reason Djemaa El-Fna had gained its name: *gathering place of the dead*. Nowadays though, the square was a hive of activity, apparently the busiest in all Africa. Angela and I were sitting in a rooftop cafe overlooking it all.

Stalls ranged from the relatively normal (shoe shiners, women selling henna patterns, spices and oils) to the rather bizarre (tiny tortoises or plastic world leaders relentlessly driving jeeps and tanks around circular tracks). And then there were the freakish items (false teeth and goat skulls). The sounds were equally exotic. They sounded like the Marrakech of my imagination — an orchestra of bizarre musical instruments with some percussion provided by the hooting of motorcycle horns. It was the perfect soundtrack to what we could see below.

Easily visible from the square, and indeed most of Marrakech, was the Koutoubia Mosque, the tallest building in the city. In fact, local statute dictated that no other building could ever be higher than the mosque, making Marrakech a distinctly low-rise city.

"I'm not sure whether I like this," I said to Angela as I poured myself another glass of mint tea. I placed the silver teapot back on its tray and took another sip. Even though I found the taste quite refreshing, the amount of sugar in the drink was too much for me.

Angela nodded absent-mindedly. I could tell she was still thinking about Muhammad, and how he'd led us on a merry old dance around the medina. "People like him just spoil it," she said. "Pressuring us into giving them money. It's not fair."

I stared down at a donkey pulling a cart filled with tin pots. Motorcycles and taxis were driving through one end of the square, the road not even marked. How people were not injured or killed was a mystery, but somehow it worked. There was a certain order to the chaos.

"I know," I said, putting my glass down next to the teapot. "But we knew this would happen. And now we know what to say if we meet another one — which we will. We've just got to be firm and tell them to get lost."

Angela nodded and took a sip of her Diet Coke.

7

To cheer ourselves up, we decided it was time to hit the famous souqs, the main tourist attraction of the city. In the centre of the square, spilling out into the medina in all directions were bewildering arrays of stalls, from tiny cupboard-sized kiosks selling nuts and spices, up to gaudily stocked fabric shops that seemed to increase in size once over the threshold.

The crowds pushed us along, and every now and again a hoot from behind would make everyone move to the side as a motorbike snaked its way past. A clanging bell indicated a donkey and cart were coming through. Bags, belts, shoes, carpets, and wooden handicrafts were everywhere to see. The smell of spices hung in the air and outside every shop sat a man waiting to pounce.

"Hello," one man boomed. He sat outside a stall peddling shoes. "I have good bargains here. I give best price! Look inside…come!"

Our eyes met for half a second and he jumped up, beckoning us towards his store. "Come in! See my quality footwear!"

We ignored him and walked on.

At a leather bag store, we decided to stop. Angela quickly spotted something she liked. The proprietor grinned a happy grin when she asked to feel it.

"This is quality leather product," he said, getting it down with his hook. "Very high quality, made only from finest leather."

Angela felt the leather and turned the bag over in her hand. "Yes, it's nice."

The man flashed dollar symbols in his eyes. "Yes, very nice!" He was grinning like a Cheshire cat.

"How much?" Angela asked.

The man shrugged and looked coy. "Madam, you give me fair price!"

Angela looked at me. I regarded the bag and decided to offer him a pathetically low amount just to see what he would do. "One hundred dirham," I said, about eight pounds.

The man's look of utter shock confirmed that the game was on, as did the uproarious laughter that followed. "One hundred dirham would not even buy a piece of rough leather! This bag is worth over six hundred dirham! But…because today has been slow day, I will sell it to you for five hundred. That is best price!"

Angela didn't say anything and so he looked at me to see what I thought about his offer. To me, £40 for a bag seemed a bit steep so I shook my head.

The man furrowed his brow and raised his palms upwards. "But five hundred dirham is best price! The leather is best quality. Please feel it, sir!"

"No thanks," I said, playing my part in this well-rehearsed haggling dance. "Come on," I said to Angela. "Let's try somewhere else."

Angela nodded and handed the bag to the man, but of course he refused to accept it. "Okay, four hundred dirham," he said. "That is final price."

Angela looked at me. I could tell she thought it was a fair price.

"No, it's too much," I said. I took the bag from Angela's hand and placed it on a nearby table. As we turned tail the man spoke again. "Okay please stop! Offer fair price! Remember, I am a humble shop keeper with children to feed!"

"One hundred and fifty dirham," I stated, looking the man in the eye.

"Three hundred and fifty!" he countered.

I shook my head. "Two hundred."

"Please, sir!" the man wailed, picking up the bag again. "The leather alone is worth more than two hundred dirham! I will lose money! The bag is yours for three hundred dirham!"

I shook my head and led Angela out of the shop. The man followed us out. "Okay, wait! Two hundred and eighty dirham."

"Two hundred," I stated again.

"Please, sir! I cannot sell the bag for such a low price. My children will starve! Meet me half way, and pay two hundred and forty."

"Two hundred and ten."

"Two hundred and thirty."

We shook hands on two hundred and twenty dirham. A fine dance it had been.

8

That night, Djemaa el Fna Square was even busier. The snake charmers had mostly departed, as had the monkey handlers, and now it was the turn of the street entertainers. Various crowds had gathered around them, and we strolled over to one group to watch two Berber musicians playing traditional instruments. One was a flute-like instrument, the other like a small banjo. The sound they created was distinctly Moroccan and pleasantly exotic.

Some crowds assembled around acrobats and storytellers; others favoured the spectacle of magicians or medicine men. Angela and I left the musicians and stopped to watch the strangest display of all. It was a man dressed as a woman cavorting and spinning like a transvestite from hell. He'd squeezed his large frame into a golden dress (adorned with dangling but highly percussive accessories) and was dancing about to a rhythm created by a second man playing a tambourine. He floated around the circle to much applause and laughter, rippling his belly for comic effect. A third man hovered at the periphery, eyeing new people to approach with his tray. After depositing a few coins, we were off towards the centre of the square, the home of the outdoor eateries.

Smoke billowed upwards from the brightly-lit food stalls, creating a translucent mist that cloaked the minaret of the Koutoubia Mosque. We chose a stall near the edge of the vast eatery section, mainly because of its spare seats. Quickly a tray of olives came, then some flat bread and a bowl of spiced sauce. A cat joined us underfoot just as the meat kebabs arrived. The meat was cooked to perfection and tasty as hell.

"Sorry, cat," I said as I took another mouthful of skewered kebab. But then guilt got the better of me. I bit off a small section and dropped it down. The tiny piece of meat disappeared and a second later, the cat resumed its imploring upwards look.

"I see the appeal of Marrakech now," said Angela, also dropping some meat down for the cat. "This square is amazing.

The food, the performers, the souq, and best of all, no unofficial guides. This is why people should come here."

9

Our riad was just minutes away from the square. The word *riad* literally translated as: *house with an interior garden*. When we'd first arrived in Marrakech, the taxi driver had stopped at the end of a narrow alleyway, telling us to follow him on foot because it was too thin for his vehicle to fit down. Unused to this sort of service from a taxi driver, but thinking it wise to heed his instruction, we followed the man until we reached a large wooden door. Entering, we couldn't believe that such a beautiful place could exist within such dimly lit alleyways. We paid the driver and he nodded and bowed, pocketing his money.

Our ground floor room was on the edge of a small courtyard. A trickling fountain lay in the centre. Our heavy wooden room door would keep out intruders, but the windows would offer no such protection because instead of glass, they utilised heavy fabric curtains. Luckily they only overlooked the central section of the riad, and not the alleyway outside.

"Well today was okay actually," said Angela, poring over the booty we'd bought in the souq earlier. Bags, shoes, belts, ornaments, and a red fez that I already regretted buying littered the room.

"Yeah, it was," I said, picking up a lamp and turning it around so I could study the work that had gone into it. The proprietor had said that four individual artisans had been responsible for it, and I had no reason to doubt him. My only concern was fitting everything into our luggage.

"And I'm glad we started in Morocco and not somewhere else," said Angela. "I think Marrakech has given us a good idea of what's to come in Africa. Come on, let's get some sleep."

10

The next morning we ventured up to the riad's rooftop breakfast area. Chattering birds and busy streets indicated that Marrakech had woken well before us. After finishing our breakfast of fried bread and delicious dips, we walked over to the roof edge. Between the satellite dishes and telephone wires, Marrakech looked ancient. It was time to head down into it.

Along a back alleyway close to the medina, we found two cats. One was a mangy-looking ginger animal chewing on a discarded chicken head, but next to it was perhaps the most pitiful cat we'd ever seen. Matted fur covered a rake-thin body, its tail blackened from all the puddles it had trailed through. But its eyes were the worst thing. One was permanently closed while the other looked like it had been gouged out. The thing's ears twitched as I bent to give it some bread. It gobbled it down in a second. I wondered how it survived.

"Hello," said a man's voice.

We turned to see a young man wearing jeans and a T-shirt. He was smiling.

"Do you need any help today? Perhaps to see the tanneries, or maybe to visit where carpets are made?"

Angela stiffened and shook her head. I shook mine too. "No, we don't need a guide, thank you. And don't bother following us please. We are fine by ourselves. Do you understand?"

The man raised his hands in acquiescence. "Of course."

We walked away, and the man didn't follow.

11

Undiscovered until 1917, the Saadian Tombs were now a major tourist attraction of Marrakech. They contained over a hundred and fifty graves of rich Moroccans.

Inside, visitors were wandering the gardens to admire the plaster archways, or else gazing at the centrepiece, the Chamber of the Twelve Pillars, the final resting place of Sultan Ahmed el-Mansour, the man who commissioned the tombs. The shaded mausoleum featured highly-decorative tiles, both on the floor and walls, as well as the twelve marble columns that had given it its name. Before French archaeologists had rediscovered the tombs, the area had been a slum area.

"Who was the sultan?" asked Angela.

We found a shaded spot where I got the guidebook out. Overhead a small lark flew past, before landing on a nearby wall. The Saadian Tombs were proving to be a peaceful oasis amid the commotion outside.

"It says he was an early 17th century sultan who died of the plague. But before that, he was good at organising battles. He spent most of his money on these tombs and on a palace."

Not far from the tombs was a rooftop terrace with a nice little cafe. As we sipped our drinks, we could see large storks sitting in gigantic nests on the top reaches of some buildings. Storks were revered in Marrakech, we knew, and harming one carried a stiff, three-month prison sentence. Just then, one flapped its long wings and took off, heading in the direction of the square.

Our time in Marrakech was almost at an end, and I asked Angela what she thought the highlights were.

"The souqs," she answered straightaway. "All that haggling and all those leather bags! I loved it. The food was good too."

I took a sip of my cola. "My favourite thing was the central square. I could've stayed there all day, just watching what was going on."

Angela nodded. "Those donkeys around the edge were so cute."

We finished our drinks and made our way back to the riad to pack. It was almost time to visit the second African nation of our tour: The Gambia.

Chapter 2: Bumster Madness in West Africa

Interesting fact: The Gambia is the smallest country on mainland Africa.

To most British tourists, The Gambia (a former British colony that gained its independence in 1965) is an easy, accessible package holiday destination. It's a step (but only a small one) above the bucket and spade destinations offered by Spain, Greece and Turkey. Oddly enough, it also has a shady reputation as a country where middle-aged white women can meet young Gambian men. Like their male counterparts who flock to the fleshpots of Bangkok, these women are the sex tourists of West Africa. Angela and I wondered whether we'd see any.

After landing at Banjul Airport, we were shepherded aboard the small minivan. The heat had definitely increased since leaving Morocco, but that was no surprise since The Gambia was firmly in the tropics.

It was good to be inside an air-conditioned vehicle. The only other passenger was a middle-aged white woman with no husband or partner in tow. She sat by herself, staring out of the window. She smiled briefly when we sat behind her.

The journey to our hotel was along a decent road, intersected by dusty tracks leading into the hinterlands. Palm trees, shacks and children playing football passed us by in a blur of colour. Roadside markets sold bananas and mangos, and every now and again, we saw goats and chickens roaming free. A few minutes later, we passed a small mosque, reminding us that The Gambia was an Islamic nation, despite its British heritage.

I removed the guidebook from my bag and looked at the map of West Africa. The Gambia was a tiny sliver of a country. It ran worm-like from the Atlantic Ocean in a horizontally east direction along the River Gambia. At its widest point, it was less than 50km wide. "The reason it's so thin," I whispered to Angela, "is because of the British. They measured how far a cannon ball could travel from the river, and that's where they put the border."

In contrast to the obvious poverty, road signs were advertising the latest Wi-Fi or mobile phone networks, of which *Africell* seemed the most popular. A short while later, we hit the outskirts of Serrekunda, The Gambia's largest town. Cars, taxis, bicycles, and of course people clogged the roads. Most of the women wore brightly coloured wraps and headwear, the men preferring jeans and T-shirts. Shops sold everything from aluminium sieves to gaudily designed beds. Most, however, specialized in second-hand car parts.

Once past Serrekunda, the van lurched to a halt outside a small hotel and the silent woman alighted. Two young black men appeared from a gate and one of them curled his arms around the woman. She seemed happy with this and allowed the men to lead her inside. Angela and I glanced at each other but said nothing. Thirty minutes later, we arrived in the small town of Bakau, the location of our own hotel. It was a large establishment full of European tourists.

2

The hotel bar advertised a happy hour between 8pm and 9pm, so Angela and I went down an hour before the rush to have a quiet drink. Unsurprisingly, we found ourselves alone with the barman.

"You are early for happy hour," he said jovially.

"I know," I said, "That's why we're here."

After getting our drinks, the barman stopped to chat. He told us the hotel had opened in 1988 after the owner had taken out a loan from the Gambian government. "It became popular and made lots of money. Rich people from West Africa came to stay, as did wealthy Europeans. But then the owner refused to pay back his loans so the government seized the hotel from him. They closed it down." The man shook his head and cleaned a glass, as barmen did across the world. "The loans were eventually taken over by a millionaire from Mali, and the hotel opened again. But the new man didn't pay the government either, so it is now owned by the department of social security."

I asked him what Gambia's neighbouring countries were like.

"Senegal is nice," he said. "I have been there many times. But Guinea-Bissau is not so good. The people there have a problem. They like to cause trouble. Not long ago, they kill their own president!"

I mentally crossed Guinea-Bissau off our list of possible side-trip destinations. Senegal sounded more promising though. I wondered whether we could possibly arrange a trip there. After all, it was only a short ferry ride away. I asked the barman about this possibility.

"Yes. A trip to Senegal is something this hotel can organise for you. They have done this many times for the tourists, and I think it can be done in one day. Reception will be able to help you, I'm sure."

We thanked the barman and finished our drinks.

3

The next morning, with a day trip to Senegal booked in, Angela and I decided to walk to the centre of Bakau. As we headed for the hotel's exit, a voice called out to us. It belonged to an overweight man lounging on a sun bed.

"You're not going out there, are you?" he said in a Birmingham accent. The man was lying next to his wife. Both were in their mid-fifties, we guessed, and looked like cooked lobsters.

I nodded. "We want to see what's around and about."

The man frowned and shook his head. "I wouldn't if I were you." The man's wife lifted her head, removed her sunglasses, and nodded in agreement.

"Bumsters," the man said ominously.

I looked at Angela, but she looked as nonplussed as I did. "Bumsters?" I said to the couple.

The man's wife spoke. "They're everywhere. Last year, we decided to go out...never again. They followed us all over the place, wanting money. Terrible experience, wasn't it, Keith?"

"Horrible."

We thanked the couple for their advice, but headed out anyway. As soon as we cleared the hotel gate, a bumster approached.

4

Bumsters, we later found out, are synonymous with The Gambia. They are young Gambian men who offer their services to any tourist who happens to wander by. In tourist areas, there might be hundreds of bumsters, most hanging around outside hotels waiting for people to leave.

"Hello? What's your name?" said the young man with a toothy grin. "Where you from? England, I bet! Do you recognise me? I work at your hotel?"

We successfully brushed him off, but the next one, a young man who seemed to favour white T-shirts, was particularly annoying. Over the next few days, we could see him a lot. He would become our Nemesis.

The further we got from the line of hotels, the thinner the number of bumsters. And half way to Bakau town, they disappeared altogether or else kept out of our way.

Bakau town was rather unremarkable, with a few ramshackle stalls, a couple of faded colonial residences, some guesthouses, a football stadium and a small collection of outdoor bars that were mostly empty. There were plenty of large vultures perched in trees, though, their unkempt scrawny necks swivelling this way and that. We stopped at a roadside bar where I bought a JulBrew, the local beer. It was time to decide where to go next.

5

The guidebook said there were two main tourist attractions in Bakau: one was the botanical gardens, which we quickly dismissed, but the other sounded better – the Kachikally Crocodile Pool.

We followed the map until we came to a track that would supposedly lead us to the crocodiles. It was a dusty, uneven orange path, bordered on both sides by shacks. I consulted the map again, looking for other ways to the pool, but couldn't see any further options.

Angela voiced her concerns immediately. "We can't go down there; we don't know where it leads."

"But this is the only way, according to the map. Besides, this track obviously leads *somewhere*. Come on, we'll be fine."

We set off, passing concrete dwellings with metal corrugated roofs. Between some of the homes, children played, and chickens pecked in the dust. Along one side of the track was a thin strip of stagnant water, most probably a drainage ditch. Flies buzzed in dark corners, but at least there didn't seem to be any bumsters.

We came to a crossroad that wasn't on the map. We stopped to get our bearings, and a small boy ran past us giggling. Another boy was chasing him. Both quickly rounded a corner and disappeared from sight. A woman sat in a doorway ahead of us cradling a baby in her arms. From somewhere came the sound of music playing through tinny speakers.

I could tell Angela wasn't happy, and to be honest, nor was I. One consolation was that the people around were paying us no heed. No one pointed or stared – even though we seemed to be the only white faces in the heart of their residential area – they were clearly used to tourists. We rounded a bend and saw a woman collecting water from a well with a hand pump. We walked past her. She didn't even glance in our direction.

"I told you we shouldn't have come down here," said Angela five minutes later. Above our heads, vultures circled in the heat of a West African sun. "If we get lost, I'm going to blame you."

I decided not to mention that we were *already* lost, the map in my hand rendered useless a long time previously. We walked on and came to another intersection, and this time turned right. I pretended to Angela that I knew where I was going, even though I didn't have a clue. Anything could happen to us in here. I thought bleakly. Angela was right. We should not have gone down the track.

"Listen," I said, signalling for Angela to stop walking. And then I heard it again. It was the unmistakable sound of a car engine. We were near a road! Angela heard it too and so we began walking, this time hurrying along the sand-covered track. Around another bend, we could see it: a main road.

"Let's leave the crocodile pool for later," I suggested.

"Yes, let's."

Back at the hotel, I read that the place we'd been in was known as Bakau residential quarter. The guidebook referred to it as a tight jumble of sandy lanes, and actually recommended it as a tourist attraction. Apparently, the homes within the quarter belonged to hotel workers, tourist guides and taxi drivers. And bumsters.

6

That evening, we went to a local restaurant that offered Italian food as a specialty. With a lack of other eateries in the vicinity, and not wanting to venture into the unknown again, especially with the dismal lack of street lighting in Bakau, we decided to try it out.

There was no one inside the restaurant except a white man sat in a far corner reading a newspaper. When he saw us, he got up and nodded. "Please sit," he said in an Italian accent. "Anywhere you like because as you can see, business is not so good."

The table we chose only had two chairs but the man pulled up a third and joined us. He told us he was the owner of the restaurant. "I don't know why I bother with this place though. I have lived in The Gambia for four years now," he told us. "And this restaurant is everything I have."

The man was clinically depressed. His face was glum and his mannerisms slow and laboured. In fact, the only thing that seemed to cheer him was talk of football, especially his home team, Inter Milan.

"So what's it like living in The Gambia?" asked Angela, breaking an uncomfortable silence.

The Italian rolled his eyes, as if to say, "Don't ask."

Another silence ensued and after a few seconds of clock ticking, I decided to tell him about the bumsters we'd encountered on the short walk to his restaurant. Suddenly he appeared interested. "What did they say? Did they mention my restaurant? Did they tell you to stay away?"

We told him that they hadn't mentioned his restaurant, and the man seemed relieved but no less dispirited.

"They are not nice people," he said. "They annoy the tourists and they annoy people like me. But who is to blame? The bumsters? The Gambian Government? Or is it my fault for coming here in the first place?"

We didn't know what to say and so said nothing. The man got up and walked back to the kitchen.

I looked at Angela. "Well he was a fun chap, wasn't he?"

"I feel sorry for him. It must be hard living here."

Ten minutes later, our food arrived. It turned out to be quite good.

7

The next day we hired a taxi to take us to the capital, Banjul. Along the way, we passed the local prison, its vulture-topped guard towers looking suitably desolate and uninviting, just as they ought to be, I thought.

Fifteen minutes later, we pulled up under the shadow of Arch 22, Banjul's most famous sight. The taxi driver said he'd pick us up in two hours.

Arch 22 was a huge concrete edifice standing at the western edge of Banjul. It had been painted a nice cream colour and featured eight sturdy columns supporting the massive arch. The government had built it in 1996 at a cost of $1.2 million to celebrate their victorious coup over the former president. The date of the coup was the 22nd July 1994, thus the name. Arch 22 also featured on the back of the 100-dalasi note, and after paying the small entrance fee Angela and I climbed the spiral staircase to the top.

The view from the top spanned much of the small capital. We could see the port in the distance, with the Atlantic Ocean just beyond it. The twin-minarets of the King Fahad Mosque, the largest mosque in the capital, stood proud, overlooking the city.

Suddenly a couple of people arrived on the viewing platform: one a large white woman wearing a sarong, the other a young black man in a tight T-shirt. Both were holding hands. We decided it was time to climb back down.

Gambia's capital was small (a population of less than 50,000) and was more like a small town than a city, but it did contain one other must-see sight: Albert Market, named after Queen Victoria's husband. With Arch 22 behind us, we walked along Independence Drive towards it.

Independence Drive was one of the main roads running through Banjul, and as Angela and I briskly headed down it, we passed the Old Mosque, the Royal Victoria Hospital and Saint Mary's Cathedral. The people along the road were going about their daily business, some of the men dressed in suits and all the women wearing dresses of vibrant colours, bright blues, green and purples. There was not a bumster in sight, and for a good ten minutes, we could wander along a Gambian street without the threat of being hustled or forced upon. That all changed in Albert Market.

8

With most Gambians not possessing a fridge, or even the electricity to power one, the women of the family had no choice but to take the daily trip to Albert Market to buy all the provisions they would need for the day. That made it a place of haggling, of noise, of jostling and unfortunately, of bumsters. They were there because of the tourists, and as soon as we stepped through the gates, Angela and I were honey to the bees.

A young man claiming to be our friend accosted us within one minute. Trying to shake him off, we entered a small clothes stall, but he simply waited outside. As soon as we left, the man doggedly followed our every move, asking question after question.

"You come to buy a belt?" he said. "Or maybe a hat? You need a hat to keep the sun off your head, man. I show you where best hats are. I can get you good deal, man. How 'bout it?"

Totally blanking him, we continued through the market, until a second bumster arrived. He too began walking with us, asking about where we'd come from and what we were doing. Then in the midst of this battle of the bumsters, a third one arrived.

The new arrival muttered something to the other two and they quickly scarpered. The newcomer flashed a plastic ID card at us and smiled. We didn't have time to read the card before he put it back in his pocket.

"I am market security," he said. "Those men were trying to bother you, but now they are gone. You have to be careful in this market; many people will try to rip you off or steal from your bag. I will look after you."

We thanked the man, but fearing he was just another bumster, albeit a much cleverer one than usual, we told him we didn't need any help. He nodded but followed us anyway, even entering shops behind us, chatting about this and that, trying to put us as ease. Sometimes he would natter with the proprietors in a language we couldn't understand. Everyone seemed to know him.

There were a few other white faces in the market too, all with bumsters in tow. We passed one elderly couple who smiled and nodded to us as their bumster led them into a small bag stall. We were like walking moneyboxes.

With no way of shaking off our bumster, we decided to ask him if the market sold any wooden carvings. It was the main reason we had come to Banjul. Quick as a flash, he nodded and led us around a couple of turns, and through a few aisles, until we came to a set of stalls selling exactly what we'd wanted.

Thanking the man for his help, we browsed through the stalls while the man waited a few feet away. After Angela had bought a couple of things, I asked him if he could show us the way out of the market. He smiled and led us there straightaway.

"Thanks," I said, wondering if this was the point he would ask for money.

"No problem, man. I hope you have enjoyed yourself in this market. Just be careful of the thieves. Have a nice afternoon."

I was shocked. It seemed we had met the only honest man in Banjul. It cheered me to know there were people who didn't just see Europeans as walking cash machines. We thanked the man and started to walk back down Independence Drive.

Twenty seconds later, we heard a voice. "I don't suppose you *could* spare a little money?" We turned to see him standing there. He'd caught us up. "It is a hot day, and I think I would perhaps like to buy myself a cold drink."

I looked at Angela. My restored faith in humanity had just been dented again.

I nodded and fished a 100 dalasi note from my wallet and handed it to him. Graciously, he thanked us and was soon gone, merging in with the crowds heading into Albert Market.

9

Back at the hotel, while Angela sunbathed on the beach, I ventured out of the hotel to visit a nearby shop. On the way, I was hassled by yet more bumsters. The first one gave up after I told him I didn't need a guide. The second one was a bit more persistent, but I eventually dispatched him when I told him I was only going to the shop, and he would get no money from me. The third bumster was my Nemesis.

"Hey man! Where you off to? The shop, huh? Let me walk with you! You lucky that I talk to you! Most people ignore the tourist, but not me! I love to talk to tourist and show them around. What you say, eh? You been to see the crocodiles yet?"

I told him I didn't need a guide, but he followed me to the shop and waited in the open doorway.

As I made my purchases, my Nemesis shouted, "Why don't you want to speak, man? It's rude not to chat!" I ignored him and paid the shopkeeper.

"Whatcha doin' tomorrow, man?" he said as we made our way back to the hotel. "Maybe see the fishermen? Or what about the day after that? You got things planned?"

"Yes," I told him. "So stop asking."

"Okay man, what about the day after that?"

I ignored him, so he asked other questions, about whether I was married and whether my wife wanted to buy some ornaments, and suddenly I began to find myself getting angry. Why couldn't this man just leave me alone? I'd made it abundantly clear that I didn't need his services, and I certainly wasn't going to hand him some money, but he wasn't getting the message.

"Go away," I said. "Please."

At the entrance to the hotel, he stopped. "I'll see you next time, man," he shouted as I walked through the gate. "I'll be looking out for you."

10

A couple of days later, Angela and I hired a green tourist taxi to take us to a nature reserve. The route took us through Serrekunda again. For some reason, our side of the highway quickly became gridlocked, a snarl of traffic going nowhere fast. The other side was empty, devoid of all traffic.

"When the president want to go somewhere," explained the taxi driver, "like maybe the airport, they close one side of the highway so he don't have to wait. It is okay that everybody else must wait though." He gestured at the traffic jam ahead.

We needed some petrol and luckily we were close to a *Total* garage. After a bit of manoeuvring our driver took us off the road and with a blur of orange dust trailing after us, we parked on the forecourt. While Angela and I waited for the driver to fill up the tank, a cavalcade of vehicles sped past on the empty side of highway.

"The president!" shouted the driver from the pump. We looked as a whirl of black limousines, jeeps and other security vehicles rolled past. And though we didn't actually see *His Excellency* himself, we knew he'd been there somewhere. Our first flirtation with an African Leader!

Abuko Nature Reserve proved to be a bit of a letdown. The guidebook claimed that birds, reptiles and monkeys would be vying for our attention, but all we saw were vultures, ants, lizards, and a small crocodile in a body of water known as the Bamboo Pool. We heard plenty of rustling though, often coming from the thick undergrowth, and sometimes we'd hear eerie screeches and hoots.

We found ourselves at an animal orphanage located at the far end of the reserve. Baboons were in cages, as were hyenas and vultures, and they all looked a little sad, especially the hyenas, lying in the dirt with their tongues flopped out. But then we saw some little brown monkeys with cute black faces. These animals were not in cages, they were roaming free. And then some more came, and soon they were everywhere.

"Come on," I said. "Back to the hotel for some rest and recuperation."

11

With Angela sunbathing on the hotel beach again, I decided to venture out to buy some JulBrew from the local store rather than pay the extortionate hotel price. I passed the couple from Birmingham again, who waved at me before resuming their baking. As soon as I stepped through the gates, my Nemesis pounced. He was still wearing the same white T-shirt as before, I noticed. This time, instead of acknowledging his presence, I completely blanked him.

"Hey where you going today? To the shop? I walk with you, man! Tell you about things in The Gambia. And then, if you like, you can give me something, so I can get something to eat? What you say?"

After five minutes of constant bombardment, I felt like I was going mad. It was like there was a grasshopper in my ear. I couldn't stand it, and so broke the number-one rule of my new tactic. "Look," I said, turning to face my Nemesis. "Will you just stop talking and leave me alone!"

He was quiet for only a second before resuming his torment, this time wittering on about Manchester United. I entered the same shop as before but this time he followed me in. "Ah, you buying JulBrew! Nice beer! Maybe I can have one?"

I bought my beer and exited the shop. A minute later, after a fresh assault on my ears, I stopped in my tracks. My Nemesis stopped too and for once, his chatter ceased. He looked at me, awaiting my announcement.

"Look, will you just piss off and leave me alone," I said angrily. "Go bother someone else because I am not giving you any money, not even one dalasi. Okay!"

To be fair, my Nemesis took the outburst well. He smiled and then asked for some money anyway.

"No!" I snapped and walked off. I was delighted when he did not follow, but this feeling of euphoria did not last long because another man immediately accosted me. This one was bigger and uglier. He tried to shake my hand, but I brushed him away and entered the hotel. The Gambia was making me more angry and bitter with every further day.

12

The next day we felt brave enough to walk to the crocodile pool again. This time, after studying the map in depth, we felt sure we knew where we were going.

"Hello! Where you going, boss lady?" said the approaching man. Angela told him that we didn't need a guide, but he persisted. "I walk with you, okay?" We ignored him and he left us alone, no doubt spying some fresh arrivals elsewhere. Oddly, my Nemesis was nowhere to be seen.

We found the same dirt track as before and quickly found ourselves in the heart of Bakau residential quarter again. The smell from the drainage ditch was putrid today, no doubt caused by the run of hot, dry days. Upon closer inspection, the dirty liquid that resided within was thick, gloopy, and hardly moving. Certain sections of the ditch were covered with corrugated metal, possibly in an attempt at quelling the worst of the stench.

As we moved further along the track, some bumsters tried their luck, but they were mostly half-hearted attempts, and then we came to our destination, Kachikally Crocodile Pool. It was down a little side track we had somehow missed a few days previously.

Inside the entrance was a tiny museum, showing various headdresses, musical instruments, and photos of the past. We quickly looked at the exhibits and then entered a small forest behind the museum that contained the famous pool.

It was larger than we expected and bright green due to algae. The surface was coated with a dense layer of lily. Gambians considered the pool a sacred place, where good luck and fertility could be gained by swimming in the water. Either that or a big bite up the arse, I wagered.

"There are lots of crocs," said Angela as we stared down into the large green pond. Most of them were in the pool itself or lounging by the side. All were covered in the green stuff, giving them an almost fluorescent look. We walked around the rim and then stopped dead.

The crocodile in front of us was huge, over two metres in length. Its mouth was agape, and its teeth were on display. It looked like it wanted to eat us. It had clearly been waiting for a stupid tourist to wander past so it could pounce. We weren't stupid though. We stood still and pondered our options. The first one was when to begin weeping.

"Imagine if it ran for us?" I whispered as we stared at the monster. We slowly backed away keeping our eyes on the reptilian creature. So far it hadn't moved from its spot. "We'd be goners."

"Is it actually real?" Angela asked quietly.

"Why don't you go over and stick your arm in its mouth to find out?"

We heard a rustling sound from behind and fearing a croc attack on our rear flank, we span around to see a smiling man. He looked like he worked in the enclosure because he was carrying a mop and a bucket. For a second, I wondered whether it was to clean up the blood from our devoured corpses.

"I see you've met Charlie," he said, gesturing at the huge reptile. "He is our friendliest crocodile. Look I show you."

The man calmly walked over to the restful reptile, put his cleaning apparatus down, and then stroked the croc's mouth. Charlie didn't move, except for its eyelids. The man invited us to do the same.

"I don't think so," I said.

"Come on, man. Charlie is friendly. And we have over eighty crocodiles in here, and none has ever attacked a person. They are too well fed for that."

"What with?" I didn't want to be the first victim of the Kachikally Crocodile Pool and so declined. Angela did too.

The man laughed and picked up his mop. "Well if you change your mind, just let me know. I am here all day."

13

"I'm going to get some more JulBrew," I told Angela. It was the next day, and I needed to restock the fridge. "So expect me to come back in a bad mood."

My Nemesis spotted me the moment I stepped foot out from the hotel. He came bounding up, smiling from ear to ear. "Hello, man!" he said as I began the regular walk to the shop. "Back for JulBrew?"

As we walked, he produced a flimsy beaded necklace from his pocket, the same sort that hung in their hundreds at every local market.

"Your boss-lady will like this for sure! It good necklace and you can have it as a gift. No strings, man. But if you want to give me a gift in return, then that would be nice!"

"No thanks," I said as I speeded up a little. "My boss-lady would hate it so just leave me alone."

But of course he wouldn't leave me alone and followed me all the way there and back from the shop. If anything, I had to admire his persistence.

14

The two young Gambian men made a beeline for the family of five sunbathing on the beach next to us. The family was from England and clearly knew the men because the father got up to greet them. His wife and teenage daughters seemed equally pleased too. After some small talk, Dad handed a couple of bags to the men. They contained things like shampoo, combs, notepads and shoes. The men gratefully accepted them.

"Tell me," said Dad, "What else can I send you from England? I'm already sending you some footballs and Manchester United kits — but what else?"

Angela and I tuned into the conversation.

One of the men thought for a moment. "Well I would like to go college to be an electrician, so mayb—"

"I'll send you some tools," interjected Mr Generous. "Screwdrivers, power tools, a whole set." He turned his attention on the other man. "What about you?"

The man paused before answering. "I would like an iPad..."

Mr Generous nodded. "Okay, an iPad. I'll send everything to your address. And once again, thank you for making our holiday so special."

After some hearty good-byes, the two men wandered off, clutching their newly received bounty.

15

The next morning was our last in The Gambia, but I still had one thing left to do. Leaving Angela in the hotel lobby, I ventured outside, in search of my Nemesis. Unlike other occasions, I spotted him before he spotted me and waved him over. He came swiftly, grinning a large grin as he did so.

"How you doing, mister!" he said, pumping my hand in the process.

I told him I was fine and asked how he was. He smiled and said he was okay and happy to be speaking to me.

I told him it was our last day in The Gambia. "We are going to Senegal later this morning, and then flying to South Africa tomorrow. But I've got something for you; a reward for your perseverance."

I gave him a few hundred dalasi and he shook my hand again.

"You have good trip, man!" my Nemesis said. "And if you ever come back to The Gambia, make sure you come to me, Mr Fix-it! You remember that. And do not listen to your hotel saying we all bad people. We like to help the tourist, that's all. See you next time."

I'd finally made peace with my Nemesis, and it felt good.

Back inside, Angela and I checked our things for the next segment of our trip. The hotel was going to look after our suitcases for the day, so all we needed were a few essentials such as sun cream, camera and passports.

"I enjoyed it here in The Gambia," I said. "But I don't think we'll be rushing back."

"No," agreed Angela. "I don't think we will."

Chapter 3: A Day Trip to Senegal

Interesting fact: Apart from a section of coastline, Senegal totally surrounds The Gambia.

With our fellow eighteen passengers, Angela and I were driven to Banjul in order to catch the morning ferry across the river. The ferry terminal was a hive of honking, shouting and dust.

The queue for cars and trucks stretched throughout the port area creating a snake of fume-belching machines. There was humanity everywhere. As we milled about waiting for the 9am ferry to arrive (it was already 20 minutes late), we had ample time to observe the hustle and bustle of our first African dock.

A couple of women were serving some sort of soup from a tiny stall. They served the broth to waiting men, accepting well-worn dalasi banknotes in return. Peddlers came up to us trying to flog sunglasses, necklaces, fake watches and other such tat. Lots of locals carried large bundles on their heads. Some men herded goats, others transported chickens by their feet, but one man had a large cart filled with huge fish that were over five feet in length. And amidst them all, children sold bags of nuts.

Suddenly our guide, a young Gambian man, beckoned us over. "We go to front of queue now. Tour groups are allowed to do this." He led us past all the waiting locals, who seemed used to the blatant queue jumping, even if we were not.

In the burgeoning heat of the African sun, we stood on the jetty where the ferry would dock. Most of us congregated in the shade provided by the waiting lorries. Thirty minutes later, the ferry approached and there was a buzz of excitement in the air. Over a decrepit tannoy system, a woman's voice ordered everyone to keep to the sides to allow departing passengers and vehicles an easy exit. Everyone squeezed back as the warning was repeated in a local language.

Almost as soon as the two-decked ferry came to a stop, the barrier lifted and the madness began. Beeping and engine sounds filled the air as cars and lorries trundled past. Clouds of noxious fumes billowed into the heavy atmosphere. A uniformed man tried to keep order, even manhandling people who seemed to be heading the wrong way, but it was like stopping a torrent with a matchstick. Eventually the last passenger departed, and the loudspeaker gave us permission to board.

If we felt hemmed in before, boarding the ferry became almost claustrophobic. We were in a mob of humanity pressed shoulder-to-shoulder, chest to back, all jostling to board. The temperature and noise were hellish, but inch by inch we edged forward, finally clambering up some metal steps to reach the upper deck. With a slight sea breeze on our faces, and a bit of room to stretch, we slowly regained our sanity.

"How old do you reckon this ferry is?" I asked Angela as we took our seats on some wooden benches. Most of our fellow tour members had already sat down or else had gathered by the rail at the edge.

Angela regarded the rusty railings, the broken benches, and the black smoke puffing out from the large upright exhaust pipe. "I'd say about thirty-nine years old."

"Nope," I said, pointing to the placard. "It's less than five years old, and it's already a banger."

Without preamble, the ferry belched a sickening blast of hot air, and we began our trip across the narrow estuary of the River Gambia.

The journey started slowly, and then continued at a snail's pace. At the mid-point the captain ordered full steam ahead, because we managed to hit perhaps two knots. As we continued the five-kilometre crossing, with Banjul fading in the haze, vendors traipsed past selling all sorts of useless tat. Lamps, toy pistols, and torches came along, as did more useful items such as nuts, boiled eggs, cold drinks, and the intriguingly named *pain balm*. The journey ended up taking an hour; a trip that would have taken five minutes had there been a bridge.

2

At the other side was the Gambian town of Barra, a hectic place of orange sand, rambling goats and wiry telegraph poles. We boarded an open-sided truck fitted with seats. As the engine wheezed into life, our guide addressed us. "We are about to set off and soon we will arrive at the Senegalese border, so I will need your passports."

We bounded off along the rutted road, leaving the small town behind, and entered scrubland and bush. Occasionally we'd pass simple concrete dwellings littered with discarded car tyres, but more often than not, the only buildings we could see were simple thatched huts. Between the bushes and homes was the orange sand. It was everywhere.

Twenty minutes later, we arrived at the Gambian-Senegal border, and my excitement was turned up a notch. Land border crossings were so much better than arriving at an airport. Men lounged about inside wheelbarrows, waiting to transport luggage between the borders. Our guide disappeared with our passports, leaving us in the truck. Like Nile Crocodiles, the teenage girls pounced.

"Cashew nuts!" they wailed en masse. There were about five or six girls, each with a tray of nuts balanced on their heads. "Only twenty-five dalasi!"

They roamed the open sides of the truck looking upwards, hoping to catch someone's eye. With no orders forthcoming, the girls changed tactics, clearly used to such reluctant behaviour. They simply laid bags of cashews on people's laps, jabbering away until a sale was made. Finally, after much persistence, they seemed satisfied and moved to the vehicle behind.

"Hello lady," said a younger girl who had just approached the truck. She was addressing the woman sitting in front of Angela and me. "Can I have your lipstick?" The woman said she didn't have any so the girl altered her request. "What about a pencil? I need it for school!" The man opposite us, who seemed to be by himself, was also being asked for things. "Get lost," he told a small boy, waving him away with a dismissive hand. Luckily the guide arrived back and we moved onwards, passing the chaotic hut that served as border control. A few minutes later, we were in Senegal.

3

Judging by Karang, the Senegalese border town we were passing through, things looked much the same in Senegal as they did in The Gambia. The road was the same, the buildings identical and, of course, the people were unchanged. In fact, the only discernible differences were the storefront signs written in French and not English, and the differently-styled vehicle number plates. More subtle differences were to do with the local currency; it was no longer the dalasi but the CFA franc.

"Senegal was colonised by the French," explained our guide, "unlike The Gambia, which, as you probably know, was colonised by the British. This explains the different official languages. But of course the people have the same ancestry and so speak the same local languages."

We passed scenes of scrubland and the occasional village. More round huts with thatched roofs made the scene look distinctly African. Whenever anyone under the age of ten caught sight of our truck, they would wave and holler at the top of their tiny voices. In England, they would throw stones and make rude gestures.

About six miles from the border, we came to our prime destination, Fathala Nature Reserve, a large conservation area where animals had been reintroduced into the wild. As we set off on our mini-safari, there was a palpable sense of expectancy, because, according to our friendly guide, antelopes, zebras, giraffes and even rhinos roamed within.

4

"Eland!" said the guide five minutes later. Our truck came to a sudden standstill, and the engine was switched off. We were on a dusty track flanked on both sides by thick scrubland and a few tall trees. Vultures seemed to favour the upper branches. Everything looked bone dry and brown, except for the odd dash of dull green from a few leaves.

The guide pointed to the left, and everyone craned their necks. Four or five large antelope were grazing in the distance, half-hidden by tall grass. Immediately, people began pointing their cameras out of the window. Unfortunately for Angela and me, we were sitting on the right-hand side of the truck, and the man opposite had hogged the whole window. He had the longest zoom lens known to man.

We set off again.

"Gazelle!" said the guide. The truck stopped, but the animals were on the left-hand side again. Mr Zoomlens quickly got into position and began firing off his shots.

When we moved off again, I turned to Angela. "When something is on our side, I'm going to block the whole window so the bugger can get a taste of his own medicine."

Angela rolled her eyes.

"Zebra!" announced the guide. "On the left!"

This is not fair! I fumed. What was it with the left-hand side's monopoly on all things safari? And if this carried on for much longer, I would get seriously pissed off. As it was, he was blocking the whole window, and we didn't see anything of the zebras. When we moved off a minute later, he sat back contentedly, studying some of the images he'd taken.

Not long after, the guide spoke to someone on a mobile phone and announced that there were a couple of rhinos up ahead. The excitement in the coach rose because we all knew that seeing a rhino was a rarity in Fathala. Mr Zoomlens was staring outside intently, and I swivelled my neck to look too. The truck slowed and then turned along the track. "There they are," the guide said in hushed tones. "Please, everybody be as quiet as you can."

The two rhinos were on the left again, but they were not far from the track. As we slowly drove forward, we could see that both were standing under the shade of a large tree. As the truck edged closer, Mr Zoomlens was already snapping away, gleefully blocking every possible sight of the mighty mammals.

I shook my head in disgust, angry at our misfortune. But just then, the track veered to the left. Mr Zoomlens looked flummoxed. A few seconds later, the truck came to a stop, and I hogged my window for all it was worth, slowly framing my shot, squaring my shoulders and swaying from side to side for good measure. One of the rhinos seemed to be looking at us, as it munched on some vegetation. It occurred to me that if it suddenly decided to charge, Angela and I would be in its bull's-eye.

But who cares! I thought gleefully. I could see the prize of Fathala, and I knew it would be infuriating the man opposite. Angela was blocking his view too, and the thought of him gnashing his teeth was almost better than the rhinos. Then, from the corner of my eye, I could see his protrusion edging over my shoulder. *Snap! Snap! Snap!* And more bloody snaps! The lens came past even further as he got more shots in. Finally satisfied, he retreated to his side of the coach, a massive grin etched upon his face.

5

As the safari continued, people grew restless. "I've had enough now," whispered Angela.

For about an hour, we'd been pummelled along dusty tracks and seen hardly anything. Fair enough, the rhinos had been great, but after the tenth antelope, it was all getting a bit tedious. Plus the sand was a pain, covering us in a thin layer of orange, getting into every crease and fold.

As we passed a huge termite mound, the truck stopped and the guide looked excited. "If we are quick," he said. "We may see giraffes! Please follow me." His comment caused a stampede, headed by Mr Zoomlens, of course. Angela and I caught the rear and soon found ourselves trampling through the dense, bone-dry undergrowth. After being cut and scratched (some of which drew blood but not tears), Angela and I stopped to assess the situation. Was it really worth all the effort to see a glimpse of a giraffe's neck? We gave up and returned to the truck.

As soon as we sat down, I saw three giraffes lolloping through the trees in the distance. They were being followed by what can only be described as a *Benny Hill* chase mob. I pointed them out to Angela and we both began laughing. We sat back and waited.

After a short while, the giraffe hunters returned. Most had scratches on their legs, and some looked out of breath. When the woman in front showed us the photos she'd managed to get, we were glad we'd returned to the truck. The images mainly showed people's heads staring at some trees. One photo had an indistinct blurred image of what might have been a giraffe.

6

Thirty minutes later, we were back at the park entrance, and it was here that I had my first interaction with a Senegalese man. He was standing outside a shop, and while everyone queued to use the toilet, I decided to buy something.

According to the large sign, his shop sold soft drinks for 1000 CFA Francs each. I walked up to the man and asked him if he had any Fanta but he didn't seem to understand. Then I remembered that Senegal was a French-speaking country, and so I pointed at the Fanta sign.

The man nodded and entered the shop, and I followed him in. After rummaging in a small fridge, he passed me an ice-cold bottle of Fanta. He then uttered something in French, which I presumed was the cost, and so I handed him a 10000 note, the lowest one I had. It was worth about thirteen pounds. The man shook his head and said something I didn't understand, and so to break the stalemate I tried to pass him the note again.

"Non!" he repeated, pushing it away.

Okay I thought. I wanted the drink, but he didn't want my money. I doubted the drink was free and so the problem obviously stemmed from the high denomination banknote. I tried to recall any basic French I knew.

"C'est pas parles Francais," I said, which caused a look of confusion on the man's face. Then he shook his head in disgust and reluctantly took my 10000 Franc note. Next he went through the rigmarole of finding some change (which involved a lengthy trawl through numerous drawers and even his pockets) before he eventually opened the safe. Finally I received my 9000 Franc change. Satisfied with my transaction, I sought out Angela and told her all about my skills in dealing in French.

She informed me that I'd said, *It does not speak French,* to the man. I nodded, thinking it had been pretty good, considering the circumstances.

7

With the time already late in the afternoon, everyone was loaded onto the truck for the journey back to the border. A mile or so before we got there, the truck took a right-hand turn along an unpaved track. Our guide explained that we would be making a quick detour to visit a local school. "Even though it is holiday time for the children, the school will open especially. I have already confirmed this."

A landscape of dry grass, occasional termite mounds and the odd thatched hut were on both sides of the orange track. Some settlements had stone wells with wooden scaffolds and plastic buckets. All had children who rushed out, shouting and waving excitedly the moment they saw us.

When we arrived at the primary school, about a hundred green-uniformed children were sitting in a large circle, merrily singing and drumming away. They were under the shade offered from some mango trees. A man wearing a pale green shirt stood in the centre; he was later identified as the Deputy Head. When we'd all gathered behind the children, he organised them into groups, some of whom danced, while others banged on makeshift percussion instruments. It was clearly a well-rehearsed show, but uplifting nonetheless.

Leaving the children in their circle, we were ushered into a nearby classroom where we sat down at the old wooden desks. The classroom itself was a bare concrete shell with gaps in the breezeblocks to allow some light through. There was a large blackboard at the front, but there seemed little else. A thin man wearing grey stood at the front and introduced himself. He was the Headteacher of the school.

"Welcome to our school," the scholarly gentleman said. "It is a school with over two hundred children from nearby villages. Some children walk one kilometre each morning, but others walk maybe two, three, and even four kilometres."

He outlined the school day for the children (start 8.30 – finish 2.00) and the subjects they taught, which seemed similar to schools in England. He said that the classroom we were in catered for seven and eight year olds, a class of 58 children.

"Fifty eight?" someone said.

"Yes, fifty eight. It is a tight squeeze."

We all looked around the small room wondering how it was possible to fit that many kids in.

The Head talked about the day-to-day battle with resources, or lack of. "The government only provides money for teachers, for chalk and for blackboards. Nothing else." He gestured around the room. "So if any of you can spare some money, then the children will be most grateful. I will leave a box by the door. But let's go back outside and see the children."

As people left, they began depositing money in the box. By the time Angela and I got to it, it was full with Gambian dalasi, Senegalese francs and a few British pounds. We congregated around the children again, all resplendent and smiling in their bright green uniforms. With the Deputy in charge, the children stood up to sing the Gambian national anthem, and everyone clapped. The show was over and we had loved it.

Now clearly the whole thing had been a PR stunt. In fact as we left the school, I saw another classroom for older children, which had a sign saying it contained only 25 children, but it didn't detract from the fact the school was severely underfunded.

After we'd climbed back into the truck, I turned to Angela. "If I was that Headteacher, I'd wait for everyone to leave and then start whipping the kids. Get back to work! Clean my office! Get me some JulBrew! Do it now! And you, Mr Deputy, split the booty into two piles. We'll have ourselves some fun tonight! Foolish tourists!"

We arrived back in The Gambia, strangely uplifted by our day in Senegal.

Chapter 4: Johannesburg to Swaziland

Interesting fact: Swaziland has the lowest life expectancy in the world at only 31.2 years.

"Give me your wallet," said the man with a knife. Angela's passenger door car was open, and the gaunt young man was waving the blade at us like a cobra. Moonlight glimmered on its edge. An accomplice stood by my door, knife in hand, staring in at me through the closed window. His eyes were yellowed but focussed.

"Come on, man. Don't make me kill your wife!" the first man snarled, flecks of spittle spraying into the car.

It had all happened so quickly. And all because of a missed turn. We'd left the highway and found ourselves driving through a rundown part of Johannesburg. Metal-shuttered shop fronts and darkened alleyways had alerted us to our mistake. When we'd stopped at some traffic lights, the two men rushed at the car.

My mouth was dry, and I was gulping air. Beside me, Angela was cowering away from the open door, shaking her head from side to side. Unable to comprehend what was happening, I could only stare at the man. Every second seemed like an hour. His eyes bulged.

"This is your last chance, man! I'm telling you, give me your wallet or else you'll both die!"

2

Except, of course, none of this happened.

But prior to our arrival into Johannesburg OR Tambo Airport, what I've described was in the back of our minds. Virtually every guidebook and internet site we'd looked at described the real possibility of being car jacked or worse. Every day in South Africa, fifty people were murdered. In the UK, it was fewer than two. And the UK has ten million more inhabitants.

Some websites warned of avoiding such-and-such a motorway exit because it would lead to a township where death was a direct possibility. Others warned not to leave any valuables visible inside a car, and to keep the glove compartment open so that would-be thieves could see there was nothing of interest contained within. I also read, more than once, not to stop at any red lights at night. Better to drive through them and pay a few hundred rand fine than pay with our lives. Another travel website warned tourists not to venture outside alone, not even for short distances, because potential muggers were everywhere, waiting, watching, seizing the chance to rob, rape, and murder.

Consider the following brutal case.

A gang of three young men enter a wealthy family's middle-class home in suburban Johannesburg. They know it is empty because one of them is the family gardener. The first thing they do is kill the family dog by slitting its stomach open. Then they wait for the family to arrive.

Dad arrives first. As soon as Tony Viana, 54, enters the front door, the men attack him with golf clubs and knives. Still alive but badly hurt, the robbers tie him up. They order Tony to tell them how to open the family safe.

Just then, Tony's wife Geraldine, 43, and their twelve-year-old son Amaro, arrive home. Leaving Dad for the time being, the robbers quickly overpower the newcomers and tie them up in separate rooms.

With his family in dire jeopardy, Tony tells the men how to access the safe, hoping it will appease them. It doesn't. After emptying it, they shoot Tony dead and go to find Geraldine. Two of the men rape her and afterwards shoot her. Only Amaro is left alive. He is in the next room, sobbing uncontrollably.

Realising the boy can identify them, one of the men runs a scalding hot bath and when it is full, drags the screaming boy to the bathroom. During their trial, one of the defendants stated, "We gagged him because he was crying. We forced him into the bath face down, knowing he would drown."

All men pleaded guilty to murder.

So why did we want to visit South Africa? Why did we feel the need to go to a country where robbers could harm us, or even murder us? It didn't sound like a fun way to spend a holiday.

3

Our journey from Banjul involved us first flying to Dakar. From there, we boarded a South African Airways flight southwards. After collecting our luggage, Angela and I stepped into the mean, nighttime streets of Johannesburg. Fifteen minutes later, we were safely ensconced inside our hotel, the aircraft-themed Protea OR Tambo. It was so close to the airport that we would see the plane we'd arrived on from the window. The room even had an airline-style gas mask in the bathroom and a flight simulator in the lobby.

"Well, it seems quite nice," Angela said, as we sipped some drinks in the hotel's bar. The weather was sunny and, as far as we could gather, there were no gunshots coming from anywhere around the local vicinity. So far, so good.

The next morning we collected our hire car in preparation for the drive to Swaziland. The vehicle was so small that we had no choice but to put one of our suitcases on the back seat.

"All set?" I said to Angela, looking around for any potential carjackers.

"I think so."

I turned the ignition and engaged the gear stick.

4

From Johannesburg, Angela and I drove east. After leaving the big city behind, our nerves settled, and we began to enjoy the journey, one mostly made up of green fields and rolling countryside. The cars travelling along with us were courteously-driven and well maintained. We saw no hostiles with guns, and not once did anyone try to ram us off the road.

Four hours later, we reached the South African border, which like many roadside borders, was an ugly collection of buildings where we had to queue with a mob of people all waiting to get forms filled in and papers stamped. Conversely, the Swazi border was highly organised and worry-free. After only a fifteen-minute wait, we were free to enter one of the smallest nations in Africa. Swaziland is about the same size as Wales.

5

Swaziland is one of three remaining monarchies in Africa (the other two being Lesotho and Morocco) and the current king, Mswati III, became ruler in 1986, aged just 18.

Mswati inherited a country with two startling truths. Statistically speaking, Swaziland, out of any country in the world, is where a person is most likely to be hit by lightning. The other fact is grimmer: over a quarter of the adult population is HIV positive – the highest rate in the world.

In 2001, to combat this deadly threat, King Mswati reinstated an old law. He banned all Swazi women aged below 18 from having sex. The king decreed that all girls under this age must wear blue and yellow tassels, effectively marking them off-limits to lusty lads. If a boy was found having sex with a girl wearing the tassels – his family would be fined one cow, a hefty price tag in a country where subsistence farming is the mainstay of the population.

Policing this bizarre law was difficult, especially when the king himself decided to marry a local 17-year-old girl (his thirteenth wife). However, to pay his dues, Mswati did relinquish a cow as remittance.

Mswati's father, King Sobhuza II, also had an eye for the ladies. Before his death in 1982, he'd married seventy women and fathered over two hundred children. As of 2012, the current ruler has only managed to sire a paltry twenty three.

6

The Swazi border town was made up of a petrol station, a line of trucks and a few small eateries, all of which we bypassed in favour of heading onwards to the capital. Billboards advertising casinos were along the roadside, as were stalls selling fruit and vegetables. Occasionally we'd pass people waiting for the minibus taxis that plied the route, always a feature of African roads.

The scenery beyond the highway was what caught our eye though: a blend of limestone rocks, torrid hills and mountains. Vegetation covered most of the land, and we couldn't get over how lush Swaziland looked. Just then the heavens opened (thankfully with a lack of lightning), and a fog descended. It took only moments for it to obscure the tops of the peaks.

"It's like the Lake District," I said as we drove up and down a winding two-lane highway devoid of busy traffic. "I can't believe it's Africa."

The Mountain Inn Hotel was located just south of the Swazi capital, Mbabane. According to its own website, it was the *'diplomat's choice for comfort and convenience.'* It certainly seemed plush from the car park. When we checked in, the lady at the desk apologised for the weather. "Perhaps tomorrow will be better," she told us. "But who knows."

We finished the evening in the Irish-themed hotel bar, where I managed to sample the local lager, Sibebe. It was delicious. The Mountain Inn was indeed a fine choice for the weary traveller.

7

The next morning we awoke to an even denser layer of fog. With the hellish sound of rain drumming down on the roof of our apartment, a dip in the pool was clearly out of the question.

The weather had actually scuppered our plans for the day, because we'd planned to visit a game reserve. But with the weather so foul, we didn't fancy sitting in the back of an open-topped jeep with only the sounds of hooves being audible through the mist. Instead, we decided to drive into the capital, which was only five minutes from our hotel.

Mbabane (pronounced m-bub-ban) turned out to be a small town flanked by some gorgeous mountains in the distance. Our arrival coincided with a partial lift in the weather, bringing colour and heat to the town.

Swaziland's capital had none of the piles of rubbish or honking traffic that seemed to plague other African cities. Instead, it had a four-lane highway cutting through well-kept, but nondescript, buildings. It had a little brown river too, overlooked by tropical, pink-blossomed trees. Even so, Mbabane was never going to win awards for its beauty and tourist attractions.

We parked outside *The Mall* shopping centre. Clothes shops, fancy eateries and coffee shops were inside, with people wandering around trying to spend the local currency, emalangeni. In one shop, I bought a newspaper called the Swazi Observer because of the headline. It read: *Prince's widow goes bananas, bolts out of mourning house, insults mourners, takes dead husband's car and runs over two people.* With a headline like that, I simply had to buy it. Another story described how a woman had used a stick to assault her 23-year-old daughter-in-law in a row over washing powder.

We stopped in a cafe where I read another juicy story. According to the report, residents of a small, unnamed Swazi town were *'grasped by fear'*. The discovery of a man's body near a river caused the fear. The victim was washed up under a bridge. Some parts of the body were chopped off. The article didn't say which bits.

But the most worrying article was on page 16. It described how a local seventeen-year-old albino girl had gone into hiding. Just days previously, someone had beheaded her 11-year-old sister and taken away the body.

The younger girl was killed because of her albino status. Her murderer would sell the body to a witch doctor, who would then prepare parts of it for sale. Many people in Africa honestly believed that albino body parts could cure them of diseases, or even prolong their lives. Recently in Tanzania, a fifty-year-old man kidnapped a five-year-old albino girl. Once he'd chopped off her limbs, he drank the girl's blood. Police soon captured him, and Tanzanian courts sentenced him to death. But that was just one case of many.

I closed the newspaper, feeling depressed at what I'd read.

8

"Let's go to Piggs Peak," suggested Angela after we'd finished our coffees. In front of her was a map of Swaziland, and she was pointing at the north-eastern edge of the country, close to the South African border. "It's only an hour away and there are lots of craft stalls to stop at along the way."

Piggs Peak (no apostrophe) was a small town named after William Pigg, a gold prospector who'd founded the settlement. Interestingly, Pigg's son ended up marrying a girl with the surname Hogg. Gold mining had brought prosperity to the town, but that all ended in 1957 when the gold ran out. Today, the main industry of Piggs Peak was logging. As we headed towards the town, foresters had already felled large swathes of forest, leaving piles of logs along the roadside.

Piggs Peak turned out to be a bit of a let down. It was a busy trading town with large groups of people going about their daily business, but not much in the way of tourist attractions. Orange sand covered the ground, and the only thing of interest seemed to be a line of small shops and a hair salon. It had a casino somewhere, but that didn't interest us either. The story we'd read in the newspaper about a woman running over her fellow mourners had occurred in Piggs Peak the previous day. With nothing much to do or see, we didn't linger and instead drove onwards.

9

"What are they doing?" I said as we rounded a bend in the road. We'd just eaten a delicious lunch in a small Swazi restaurant, with a view over a deep green canyon. Weaverbirds had busied themselves in nearby trees, and a large blue-headed lizard had patrolled the grass. To the north, we'd been able to see into South Africa and the start of Kruger Park.

I slowed the car down. A thick forest of evergreens covered both sides of the road. Evidently, the loggers had yet to move into this area. What caught our attention, though, were the six small children standing at the side of the road. They seemed to be dancing. A teenager was with them, stood to one side, beckoning us to stop.

"I know about these!" Angela said excitedly. "They're banana dancers. Small kids dressed up in banana leaves who dance for passing cars in the hope of getting a bit of change. I read about them last night."

We stopped the car and watched the troupe for a minute or so. Mostly their routine involved clapping their hands and kicking their feet, but it was entertaining enough for us to give them a handful of coins when they had finished.

10

"How are you today, sir?" asked the young Swazi policewoman who'd just pulled us over. It was our last morning in Swaziland, and we were en route to the Swazi border so we could continue to Durban before nightfall. I'd just driven around a bend in the road when the lady in question, together with a colleague (armed with a speed camera) flagged us down from their hiding position inside a bus stop.

"I'm okay," I said smiling. "Is there a problem?"

The woman nodded. Around her neck was a whistle. "You were exceeding the speed limit."

I turned to Angela, who looked mildly amused but offered no sympathy. I turned back to the officer.

Buggeration, I thought bitterly. Speeding in Swaziland! Mustering the most shame-faced expression I had at my disposal, I told the officer I was sorry and added that I would pay more attention to my speed from now on. She nodded but asked me to get out of the car. "You must come to camera so you see for yourself how much you were exceeding the speed limit."

I nodded and climbed out, following the officer to the bus stop. True enough, the camera had recorded my speed as I'd come around the bend. I had been doing 71km/hour in a 60km zone. Wondering when I would receive my beating, I waited.

"You pay fine now," said the male officer, already writing something on a notepad. When he finished he passed it to me. It was a fine for 60 emalangeni, less than a fiver. Not bad, I thought. In the UK, it would have been sixty quid! After handing over the money to the extremely cordial and professional police officer, he passed me a receipt.

"Now we check car," said the lady officer.

We both walked back to the hire car, and the woman asked me to climb in. First she got me to start the engine, to test the windscreen wipers, indicators and brakes. While I did so, she circled the car, checking that everything was in fine working order. Everything was and so she came up to my door and leaned into the open window. "Ooh-ta," she said.

I looked at the woman blankly, and then at Angela, who merely shrugged.

"Sorry, what?" I said to the police officer.

"Ooh-ta," she repeated.

"Ooh-ta?"

"Yes. Ooh-ta."

What the hell did she want me to do? I shrugged my shoulders and shook my head. From the corner of my eye, I could tell Angela was finding the whole charade highly amusing.

"Press ooh-tah!" the officer said, tutting, pointing to the middle of the steering wheel.

Ah, it all made sense now. I pressed the hooter and the woman nodded, indicating that I could drive off. Armed with my first-ever speeding ticket in over twenty years of driving, courtesy of the Swaziland Big Bend Police Station, we drove onwards towards South Africa with Durban on the horizon.

Chapter 5: A Daytrip to the Kingdom in the Sky

Interesting fact: Lesotho is the only country in the world that lies entirely above 1000 metres.

Bound for Durban, we drove through game reserves, but saw no hide or hair of any wild animals, except for a few ostriches. Once again, the roads were safe and the drivers considerate, and seven hours after leaving Mbabane, we arrived in South Africa's third-largest city.

Originally called Port Natal by the British, Durban was home to half a million people, with almost a third of them being from Indian stock. When British settlers had noticed bountiful sugar cane to be harvested, they had transported Indian workers across the ocean to toil in the fields, most of them working a twenty-five-year contract. Understandably, after their tenure was up, many stayed, bringing their wives over to live with them. Today, Durban has the largest population of Indians outside the sub-continent.

After checking into the hotel, we were off on foot exploring the beach. The sun was out, and it felt hot. "This isn't what I expected," Angela said, as we walked along Durban's famous sea front. It was full of amusement arcades and funfair rides.

Down in the surf I noticed a few boarders were braving the waves, and on the beach and promenade, kids had packed out the sand, screaming and laughing as they jumped into open-air pools.

"It just looks a bit tacky," continued Angela. "Look at the hotels – they look like they were built in the 1960s."

Before arriving in Durban, we'd both seen photos of the city, some of which had wowed us. Aerial shots showcased a blue ocean lapping up against a golden expanse of sand, all with a backdrop of tall, striking skyscrapers. But up close and personal, Durban was a bit down at heel, grotty even. And the number of armed police officers was another worrying aspect. Neither of us could recall being somewhere with such a high police presence.

We continued along the seafront, passing tourist stalls that sold the usual mixture of African masks, bowls and carved wooden figures, but we didn't stop to buy anything. Instead, we veered away from the beach and found a supermarket in the town centre. Inside, manic Coca Cola purchasing was going on. Shoppers were filling their trolleys with large bottles of the drink, and the supermarket clearly couldn't cope.

"Tell them there is no more," said one harassed man who I presumed was the manager. He was speaking to one of his underlings, who looked equally as stressed. "Tell them it has run out!" As soon as his minions had stocked a shelf, it disappeared into the waiting convoy of trolleys.

"What's going on?" I remarked to Angela as we tried to squeeze through the melee. We simply couldn't fathom it. Coca Cola had taken over the supermarket, as if the dark liquid's properties were the magic elixir of life. Coca Cola-laden trolleys were blocking all the aisles (not to mention clogging up the checkouts), and so we left the madness, heading back to the hotel just as a storm began.

As night fell, the tempest raged, developing into an almighty thunderstorm that brought zigzags of lightning down, like special effects from a Frankenstein film. We closed the curtains and packed our bags for our trip to Lesotho.

2

South Africa surrounds the tiny Kingdom of Lesotho (pronounced Liss-ooh-too). If a map of South Africa were turned upside down, then its outline might resemble the side profile of a leopard's head. So going with this scale, Lesotho would be the eye – that's how small it is. Nevertheless, it still manages to squeeze in over two million people, most of them in the west of the country, where the capital Maseru is located.

Lesotho had been a British protectorate until it gained independence in the 1960s. Living off profits made by its natural resources, namely diamonds, water and agriculture, the fledgling nation soon began to accrue money. As a result, the government ploughed 13% of its GDP into education (the UK puts half that amount in), meaning that Lesotho has ended up as one of the most literate nations in Africa.

Our day trip to Lesotho began with a 6.30 am pickup. After driving north for three hours, we arrived in the South African town of Underberg, a cattle and dairy community located in the foothills of the Drakensberg Mountains.

Underberg's second source of income was tourism. Backpackers were everywhere, most of them perusing signs outside hiking shops or poring over large maps.

Underberg was actually a nice town with a lot going for it. While we waited for the next segment of the trip to begin, we had a bit of a wander around, finding a cafe along the street, as well as a few craft shops. Compared to Durban, Underberg was quaint and welcoming.

3

"Hi, I'm Steve," said the young man leading us to the 4x4 required for the upcoming journey. As part of our trip, Angela and I would be heading upwards along a notoriously dangerous mountain trail, where loose gravel could send us to an untimely end. Half way up the trail was the South African border, and at the top was the Lesotho border. The trail leading between them was called the Sani Pass.

Steve looked about thirty and told us he'd been a driver and tour guide for seven years. "I'll be your driver on the way up to Lesotho and hopefully on the way back down as well, unless we die before we get there!"

As people nervously laughed, I regarded the other five people in our group. There was a young South African couple, an Australian woman in her sixties, and two Swiss men in their forties who seemed to be backpacker types. We all climbed into the vehicle and buckled up for the ride ahead.

"The journey will take a couple of hours, even though it's only thirteen kilometres in total," said Steve. "But that's because we'll be climbing to over 4000ft. Along the way, we'll have a couple of stops so you can take photographs. If everyone's happy, we can go." With that, the gear was cranked forward, and we spluttered off on our uphill adventure.

4

The Sani Pass tour was clearly a popular one, at least judging by the number of other 4x4s plying the same route. Steve seemed to know most of the other drivers, all professional mountain drivers bound together by a common danger. He waved or beeped his horn every time he recognised someone.

Quickly, the road turned into a rocky path skirted on both sides by mountainous scenery. Baboons were out and about on the slopes, and Griffon vultures were riding the thermals way above our heads.

As we snaked around a bend with a sheer drop on one side, Steve asked if anyone was afraid of heights. "Because if you are, then just close your eyes for a minute. The feelings of dread will disappear. I know this, because I'm doing it right now!"

Every so often, a white minibus taxi, crammed with local people would either overtake us or else squeeze past on its downwards journey. "These guys," said Steve, "are fearless. They come up and down here all day with their cabs filled with people, luggage, and sometimes even sheep. It's all they know. But they sure can drive."

After an hour or so of jolting and juddering (which Steve called the African massage), we reached the first border control, this one on the South African side. It was basically a hut with some toilets and a large flag flapping in the mountain breeze. The customs official stamped us all out of South Africa, and we boarded the Land Rover again.

"Right!" said Steve with obvious glee. "This is where the real fun begins. The road we've been on was a smooth highway compared to what's coming. We'll be going around hairpin bends with death-defying views, and gravel will slip beneath the wheels. I took my mother up here once, and it's the only time I've heard her swear!"

We all gripped the sides as the vehicle moved off.

5

Steve was right: the road, if you could even call it that, was nothing more than a mountain goat trail. Large boulders littered the dirt track, and one in particular blocked most of the path ahead. As Steve squeezed past, he stopped and pointed at the pair of shoes beneath it. They were poking out the end, suggesting a squashed body lay hidden underneath. Someone had painted RIP on the side of the rock with yellow paint.

"Yeah, a sick joke, I know," laughed Steve, battling with the gear stick and clutch. "But actually, you guys have really lucked out with the weather today. Yesterday was terrible. Lots of people cancelled because of the rain."

The gradient of the twisting climb got worse. At one point, we began to roll backwards with a hellish spin of wheels. With a Land Rover full of stricken tourists, Steve merely laughed and brought us to a halt. "This makes it more interesting doesn't it?" He manoeuvred the vehicle into a new position, and then we were off, engine grinding as we gathered pace on the edge of the precipice. By my side, Angela looked terrified, but a second later, we were through, careering up and around a further bend.

"This reminds me of a joke by Eddie Izzard," said Steve. "In it, he's talking about his grandfather. When it's my time to die, he says, I want to die like my grandfather did – totally asleep and in peace. Not like the screaming passengers in the back of his bus."

Eventually we arrived at the top of the pass, a sparsely populated settlement with a collection of traditional round huts, a border shack and a long building claiming to be the highest pub in Africa. We climbed out of the Land Rover and immediately felt the chill in the mountain air. In the distance, a couple of local men on horses were galloping off into the rocky hinterlands. When we'd been stamped into Lesotho, we drove the short distance to one of the huts.

6

"This village is a Lesotho sheep-shearing village," explained Steve. "The people who live here lead a simple life, but the village elder has agreed we can visit as long as we show respect to his people."

The hut wasn't large, but it did have a selection of beer crates arranged for us to sit down on. A woman with a baby tied to her back hovered in the doorway.

The only light was coming from the open doorway, and it took a few moments for our eyes to adjust to the dimness. In the middle of the floor was a selection of handicrafts that Steve said the women of the village had made. "And though these curios don't look like much, it will have taken one of these women a couple of days to make, so if you buy anything, it will be greatly appreciated."

When we'd all settled down, Steve went up to the woman. She clearly knew him because she smiled when Steve tickled her infant under the chin. He then sat down and addressed us.

"Up here in the mountains there is no crime. If anyone is caught stealing, they are sent out of the village and can never return. They will not be able to join any other village so will have to live in the mountains alone. This is too much to bear for these people – to be separated from their family and their animals – so that is why they commit no crime. Simple, eh?"

In the lowlands of Lesotho, we were told, it was a different matter. "Maseru, the capital, has all the same problems as any other African city. It has crime, it has poverty, and it has a corrupt government. There is no strict village kinship there. If someone is thrown out of the family home, they simply move in with a friend, or end up begging on the streets. Up here in the mountains, as you can see, the people are much happier."

Steve was right. The women we had seen had all been smiling, and even the men on horses had seemed content with their lot.

Steve paused for a moment, looking at a few of us. "And I know what some of you are thinking. How could people live like this, with no shops or TVs, and no cars? But do you know what they say to me? They tell me that when they meet people from the city, all they see is worry on their faces and wrinkles on their foreheads. And if you think about it, this is so true. Up here, these people have no bills to pay, no taxes to worry about, and they have all the food they want. They also have something a lot of us seem to have given up. They have their family. All members of the family live in the village, and it's rare for someone to leave. When I tell them I only see my parents twice a year, they think I am a poor man, and maybe they're right."

After giving us some food for thought, it was time to sample some of the real stuff on offer. The woman with the baby stood up, walked over to a black pot, and removed the lid. Inside was some bread that we were all allowed to sample. It was delicious and still warm, heated by sheep dung no less. Next, after sipping some traditionally-made beer (which tasted like a combination of wine and petrol), we looked at the goods on offer in the middle of the hut. They were a mixture of woven baskets, coasters and a collection of things that resembled large tea cosies. We felt compelled to buy a few items, but none of us minded.

At the highest pub in Africa, I bought myself a can of the local beer, Maluti, which was nice and refreshing. Even though it was fairly nippy, the seven of us, plus another few tour groups, congregated outside to admire the view. Crags and cliff faces on the side of the rolling Drakensberg Mountains, punctuated every now and again by clumps of fiery red and yellow flowers, stretched for miles in every direction. Two boys sat on a ledge not far away, both wrapped in thick cloaks and wearing green wellies on their feet. After perhaps half an hour, it was time to leave. We crammed ourselves into the Land Rover for the drive back down the Sani Pass. It was time to go back to South Africa.

7

"I really enjoyed that," said Angela in the hotel bar that night. From start to finish, the Lesotho day trip had taken 12 hours. "I enjoyed it because it was so different. To see how those people lived up there and how happy they were. And the journey up and down the Sani Pass! I loved it!"

I nodded. The whole trip, though expensive, was well worth the early start. Lesotho was truly a Kingdom in the Sky.

After finishing our drinks, we returned to our room to pack for our flight the next day. It was time for the final stop in Southern Africa: Cape Town.

Chapter 6: The Cape

Interesting fact: Cape Town was originally called the Cape of Storms.

Our flight from Durban delivered us into a city bathed by the warm glow of summer. Both Angela and I were in a fine mood as we jumped in a taxi to the hotel. Soon we were passing some of the shanty dwellings that always seemed to be in the news for various unsavoury reasons. Twenty minutes later, we were standing on the balcony of our hotel, revelling at the amazing view. With the ocean less than a hundred metres away, and a majestic view of Table Mountain in the distance, it was perhaps the finest view we had seen from any hotel we'd stayed in.

Angela clapped her hands with glee. "I think I'm going to like Cape Town."

2

The next morning, Angela and I decided to walk from our hotel to the Victoria & Alfred Waterfront. The seven-kilometre route would hopefully be a leisurely morning stroll.

Half an hour later, we found ourselves traipsing past shipping warehouses, and crossing over rusty railway lines. A few people passing in cars stared, but no one gave us any trouble. Besides, the sun was out and we were enjoying ourselves. We could see Table Mountain ahead of us and we knew we were going in the correct direction.

Until 1988, the Victoria & Alfred Waterfront was full of abandoned harbour buildings, with much of it cut off from the actual city due to freeways and roundabouts. Not that people wanted to visit it anyway; it had been a wasteland of derelict fishing boats. Then the Mayor of Cape Town cooked up a plan to redevelop the waterfront, resulting in the construction of shops, bars and restaurants, all under the shadow of Table Mountain. It is now a major tourist attraction.

One and a half hours after leaving the hotel, we arrived. A large Ferris wheel, called the *Wheel of Excellence*, towered above it all. It was hard to imagine the area we were standing in ever looking derelict.

"Look!" said Angela, peering over a railing into the water. A couple of seals were frolicking in the sea, disappearing for a few seconds before curling playfully back to the surface. "They're so cute!"

We left the seals with their audience of perched gulls, and began a wander around the waterfront. Plenty of other tourists were about with us, many of them waiting for boat rides or doing a bit of shopping. Lots of boat rides went to nearby Robben Island, the place where Nelson Mandela had once been imprisoned for eighteen years.

Deciding to save a boat trip until a later date, Angela and I entered a shop selling wooden carvings and painted ostrich eggs. While Angela looked at some small carvings of hippos, I decided to take a photo of a large zebra skin hanging near the door.

A man tapped me on the shoulder. "No photo," he said.

I lowered my camera and faced the man. He was a large individual who reminded me of a nightclub bouncer. "Why not?" I asked.

The man pointed at a sign. It read: *Please don't take any photos inside this shop – for security reasons*. "That's why," he said.

Shaking my head, I put my camera away unable to comprehend the stupidity of this rule. What security reasons? How could taking a photo cause any potential danger? *Hello MI5, yes, I have managed to infiltrate the carving store. I got the photo of the zebra skin and plastic snowstorm depicting Table Mountain. I shall send the evidence in microfilm.* It was total idiocy and buffoonery of the highest order.

3

"Cape Town is nicer than Durban," I said the next day. We were once again back at the Victoria & Alfred Waterfront, apparently the place in South Africa with the highest concentration of foreign tourists. "There's not even a hint of menace about the place."

Once again, we sought out the seals and there were plenty of them lounging about in a special fenced-off area or playing in the harbour. We decided to go for some lunch on the waterfront, even though we knew it would be expensive. "Who cares?" said Angela as we spied a suitable establishment overlooking the harbour. "We're only here once."

As it turned out, the prices were not that bad, and Angela's ostrich steak looked delicious. Unlike what we'd imagined, it was a dark meat and nothing like chicken. She offered me a forkful, and the taste surprised me – it was like beef, only nicer.

"I've read about ostrich meat," Angela told me, cutting a chunk off for herself. "It's better than beef because it's low in cholesterol. It's got less fat than chicken." She put the fork of meat in her mouth and tasted it. A few seconds later, she nodded appreciatively. "This is good!"

In the centre of Cape Town was a large Edwardian building called City Hall. Built with limestone imported from Bath, it was where Nelson Mandela had made his first public speech after his release from prison in 1990.

Angela and I thought it was time to pay a visit to Table Mountain. In the distance, we could see a cable car making its way up, and so, after consulting the map, we decided to walk to the lower station. This proved to be an error.

4

At first, the walk towards the cable car station was leisurely, passing through a leafy promenade with a lovely little park next to it. The ever-so-slight incline was hardly a taxing walk and, to be honest, it didn't look that far to our destination.

"I'm so glad we didn't get a taxi," I said as we walked together in some shade offered by the trees lining the edge of the walkway. "This is much nicer."

Twenty minutes later, I would've killed for a taxi. The park had disappeared, and we were climbing up a residential street lined with expensive-looking dwellings. The trees had long gone, and the sun was blazing down upon us without mercy. Without warning, the road's incline got steeper, and soon I was walking at such an angle that my arms were almost touching the ground. My lungs were on fire, and my muscles were crying out in pain. Through the haze of the day, my mind suddenly delivered something worse. We were only half way towards the cable car. I stopped to pant and gibber.

"Oh, stop moaning," Angela said. "It's not that bad, and besides, it was your idea to walk."

Angela was not suffering anywhere near as badly as I was. All the keep-fit classes she'd been attending were now paying off. I grumbled something but carried on walking. If this was what exercise felt like, I promised myself never to attempt it.

Then a more worrying thought rose to the surface of my mind: it was to do with how much water we had. I checked my bag and found we only had one small bottle between us, and half of that was gone already.

I felt the first stirrings of alarm, especially as there were no shops in sight. I wondered whether we should knock on someone's door, but the large spiky gates, and signs warning trespassers away, put me off.

"Angela," I croaked, showing her the bottle. "This is all we have."

Angela stopped to look at the contents and shrugged. "That's enough. We'll be fine."

Dragging my limbs forward, I seriously doubted it. Especially since the closer we got to the damn mountain, the bigger it looked. I now had to crane my sweat-drenched neck to see the top.

We passed the last house, and incredibly the gradient increased more. I spun around to look at how far we had come, but ended up depressed because it looked so pitiful compared to how far we still had left to go. Even Angela was acknowledging that the path was a little steep now. Onwards we climbed, leaving the city limits behind, heading into scrub. And then cruelly, the path ended.

"Damn!" I screeched, collapsing on the stony ground. I was soon up again when I discovered how hot the ground was. Plus I'd noticed lots of ants. In front was a ghastly sight: a rubble-infested trail leading into thick scrub. A large gate blocked it.

"Damn you!" I said again, feeling the cracks in my lips with my bone-dry tongue. I shook my fist at the gate. "Damn you to hell!"

Angela smiled and asked for the water. After we'd both taken large gulps, there was less than a quarter left. Both of us stared upwards.

5

"This is the stupidest thing we've ever done," I gasped, as we lumbered towards the gate. A notice on it read: *No Entry*, but we stumbled past it regardless.

I could just make out the cable car station in the distance, almost a mirage to my salt-caked eyes. In the bushes, I was sure I could hear the hiss of puff adders watching our faltering steps. We were on the side of a hill that no sane person would ever consider. If we had caught a taxi, we would have been at the station ages ago.

Now down to the last mouthful of water I began to succumb to delirium. All I needed was to lie down and stroke the snakes. Then I could close my eyes. I told Angela that I thought I was going to keel over, perhaps even perish on the slopes of Table Mountain, but she told me to stop being so dramatic.

But it was true! I *did* feel weak, and the thirst! Oh, the bloody thirst! That was the worst thing about it all! With my final mouthful of water gone, it was only a matter of time before I submitted. All I could concentrate on was putting one foot in front of the other, in front of the other, in front of the other...

Miraculously, after an hour and a half of uphill mountaineering in the heat and sun, without water or appropriate footwear (Angela was even carrying a shopping bag), we reached base camp. Rushing like mad people with unhinged brains, we staggered towards a stall selling drinks. After barging my way to the front, I bought two each. I downed both of mine in seconds and after giving Angela hers, I went to buy more. It was only after drinking almost a litre and a half of fluids in less than five minutes that I began to regain some sort of sanity.

It was then we noticed the queue. Hundreds of people were snaking along the road, all waiting to enter the cable car station.

"Bugger that," I said.

Angela nodded. "If that's what the queue is like down here, imagine what it will be like up there…"

So, after a few minutes of rest and recuperation, we decided to return to the Waterfront. We had scaled the North Face of the mountain, but the final hurdle had defeated us.

6

The next morning, Angela and I were back at the Victoria & Alfred Waterfront in search of a boat trip. There were plenty of touts offering such trips. The one we chose was a tour of the harbour, lasting one hour.

As we set off, the wind whipped up and I soon lost my cap. Even so, the views of Cape Town were well worth the loss. On our left-hand-side was a billowing curtain of cloud falling over the edge of Table Mountain; it was like watching a waterfall in slow motion. We powered past the main football stadium of Cape Town, and behind it was the cable-car station from the previous day. It was only a third of the way up the bloody hill.

Suddenly, out of nowhere a couple of playful dolphins appeared. We'd been told that seeing dolphins was a possibility, but this pair was coming straight towards the boat. In the surge to get the best view, Angela managed to squeeze into a prime position, and so I passed her my camera.

"Film them," I ordered.

Angela nodded and pointed the camera over the side. Through gaps in people's shoulders, I could see one of the dolphins arcing out of the water, and it was so close! I couldn't wait to see the footage Angela got. People oohed and ahhed as the dolphins flipped over and dived downwards.

"It's not my fault!" Angela said, as she passed me the camera back. "I couldn't tell whether it was on or off because of my sunglasses."

We watched the short segment she'd managed to capture. It was one second of blue sea followed by half a second of someone's feet.

"Well," I said. "I think I'll send this off to the *Discovery Channel.* I'm sure they'll want to purchase such exciting footage."

7

Our short trip to the Southern tip of Africa was over. And so what did we think? To be truthful, the media hype over violent crime had affected our travels somewhat. We had eyed some people with suspicion even though we'd had no real reason to do so. But unfortunately, South Africa *does* have violent crime and sometimes tourists *are* targeted. The difference between the 'haves' and 'have nots' in South Africa is vast, and if a tourist is foolish enough to venture into a non-touristy part, then there is a good chance of them being robbed or worse.

Even the central (i.e. touristy) part of Cape Town is not free from crime. According to a police report from 2011, four robberies a day took place, some of them in broad daylight. A favoured spot for muggers was the lonely trails leading up to Table Mountain. We only found this out after our return to the UK. It seemed Angela and I had been lucky that day.

That evening, our last in South Africa, we packed our things for the final stop of our first African adventure. We were flying out of Cape Town and heading northeast (via Qatar) to the Seychelles. We had enjoyed South Africa, but it was time to leave.

Chapter 7: Paradise in the Indian Ocean

Interesting fact: the world's biggest tortoise lives in the Seychelles.

As we wandered along the jungle trail, passing exotic fruit trees and herbal leaves, we heard the strange sound. It was like a man straining to do hefty work, only not a normal man: a monster man.

"*Uggghhhh!*" the thing groaned before becoming silent for a few seconds. Angela I looked at each other, wondering what it could be.

"*Uggghhhh!*" it went again, a reverberating sound straight from hell. It was louder this time.

"What is it...?" I whispered as we passed under a breadfruit tree. It was a wonder the fruit weren't shaking from all the noise. "And where's it coming from? It sounds like a dragon giving birth."

We were inside a huge herbal jungle. Along its many trails, tourists could stop and stare at the different plants and indigenous creatures native to the Seychelles. But what else lurked behind the thick foliage, we wondered?

As we edged through the jungle, we tried to sense any indication that the beast might be nearing, but thick leathery leaves blocked any view beyond a few feet. *"UGGGGHHHH!"* it suddenly roared. It sounded like it was just across from us.

And then, we came to a clearing and could see the source of the terrible sound. Immediately the straining moans made perfect sense. It was a giant tortoise on top of another giant tortoise, and both were engaged in an act of pure reptile coitus. Every time the male heaved forward, he made the tortured sound: mouth agape, eyes half-closed and tongue lolling over the side of his chops.

"Jesus bloody Christ!" I said, staring at the sordid scene. The female tortoise looked uninterested by the whole proceedings, as did the other tortoises in the enclosure, but the male on top was heaving like an old man doing a press-up.

"UGGGGGGHHHHH!" it bellowed again, hoisting itself forward. Beside me, Angela was laughing, while the deep resonant sound cascaded through the rainforest.

"I'll tell you something," I sniggered as we walked to the edge of the enclosure. "This bugger has got some stamina. He's been going at it for ages. He looks like he's about to pass out."

And then we noticed that things were not going according to plan for the randy reptile. His female companion had pressed her shell hard to the ground, effectively staunching his cold-blooded advances. After another couple of heaves, he gave up and simply collapsed on her back, neck pulsing and tongue flopping. The jungle returned to its normal state of chirping and wind rustling. The monster had been felled.

2

The Seychelles was without doubt the most beautiful place Angela and I had ever visited. As well as its miles of stunning beaches (all surrounded by the clearest blue ocean imaginable), it had lush rainforests that rose into the highlands of the interior, and a quaint and colonial capital city, Victoria, a place so small that it was possible to bypass it in only a few minutes. But the piece de résistance had to be the island's extraordinary and unique granite formations. They created a vision of a pure beach paradise.

As dawn broke over heaven, Angela and I touched down on Mahe, the largest island in the Seychelles. The heat and humidity hit us as soon as we left the aircraft. Then, after receiving possibly the greatest passport stamp ever (in the shape of the famous Coca de Mer nut), a man called Bernard picked us up and led us to his taxi. As we drove northwards, he began explaining the ins and outs of life on the Seychelles.

"The official language is Creole," Bernard told us. "But English and French are widely understood. There are no poisonous snakes or monkeys on the islands, but you will see lots of bats and lizards."

Bernard told us that the fruit bats were seen most commonly at dusk, or sometimes on the menu in the Seychelles.

"The menu?" I asked. "People eat bats?"

Bernard nodded. "Curried or grilled are best. But you need to be careful with the bones. They have more bones than some fish. Bat tastes delicious though."

While we digested this morsel of culinary horribleness, we stared outside to catch fleeting glimpses of perfect beaches dotted with spectacular granite rocks. They looked like the nesting place of dinosaurs. We really were in paradise, I thought. Even if the locals liked to eat bats.

3

It was still early morning when we arrived at the outskirts of Victoria. Schoolchildren merrily walked along the side of the road, whilst buxom African ladies, wearing colourful dresses, waddled with them, large grins upon their faces. Young adults sat chatting in bus stops or else listening to MP3 players, waiting for blue Tata buses to pick them up. Tiny stores by the side of the road displayed Seybrew signs or cell phone information, and before we knew it, we were past the town and threading our way upwards along a winding mountain road.

Our place of stay was located on the northern tip of the island, an area of dense jungle overlooking the ocean. When we climbed out of the car, we could see a few fruit bats flapping their gigantic leathery wings above the canopy. Vivid red finches and squawking mynah birds paraded themselves lower down. The Seychelles could not stop impressing us. With a wave, Bernard was off, heading back to the airport to pick up more passengers.

Our bungalow had an eye-watering view of the ocean outside and an eye-catching green and red-speckled gecko inside. "Wow," said Angela, a word she would say many times over the next few days. "The Seychelles is *bloody* gorgeous."

4

The next day we jumped in a hire car and drove the short distance to Victoria. In the centre of the capital was its famous clock tower, which looked well kept, considering it was over a hundred years old. It reminded me of a small, white Big Ben. As well as telling the time, the clock functioned as a mini roundabout. Independence Avenue and Albert Street, the main drags of the town, crisscrossed it.

Small supermarkets, numerous trinket shops and a whole line of household goods stores were the mainstay of downtown Victoria. The number of mop buckets and colanders for sale made us quickly realise that the capital of the Seychelles was catering for its locals rather than its tourists.

Victoria did boast a couple of museums, an old colonial Court House, a couple of cathedrals and even a Hindu temple (which looked like it belonged in the bazaars of Old Delhi), all conveniently located close together. We came to the strangely named Selwyn Selwyn-Clarke Market (named after an old British governor of the Seychelles), an establishment full to the brim with mangoes, bananas, jackfruit, pumpkins, lettuces, purple aubergines and, of course, fish. Rotund ladies presided over most of the produce while their men folk whipped up sales in the fish stalls.

Half an hour later, we were enjoying a coffee in the News Cafe, a second-storey establishment overlooking Albert Street. I picked up the *Seychelles Nation*, a local English-language newspaper because of its headline: *Day 104 for Seychelles Fishermen*. In November the previous year, Somali pirates had kidnapped some local fishermen and had taken them to Mogadishu. Three months on, their fate was still unknown.

Pirate activity around the Seychelles was harming the local economy, especially the fishing industry. With fishermen understandably reluctant to venture into the open seas, fish stocks began to run low. As a result, fish prices had risen, so people had less money to spend on other things. To combat this, various nations offered the Seychelles some pirate-busting aid. Mostly, this amounted to sending warships to patrol the islands. A few pirates were captured, and then a few more, and before long, the Seychelles found itself overrun with the buggers.

As a result, the Seychelles became a world leader in prosecuting Somali pirates, jailing most of them after speedy trials. The upshot was that one seventh of the prison population in the Seychelles is made up of convicted pirates.

5

In the 17th century, the Seychelles had also been a hotbed of pirate activity. In fact, historians believe pirates were among the first Europeans to visit the unpopulated and then unnamed islands, using them as a stopover on their pillaging routes across Africa and Asia. One of the most famous pirates to land on the Seychelles was a Frenchman named Olivier Levasseur.

Like any pirate worth his salt, Levasseur wore an eye patch. He was also highly intelligent and skilled in the acts of piracy. After hooking up with a couple of English pirates called John Taylor and Edward England, the trio plundered their way around Madagascar and East Africa, becoming fairly rich in the process. Eventually though, Lavasseur and Taylor grew tired of Edward England and marooned him on Mauritius. The remaining pair then went on to commit their most audacious act.

They already knew that the Portuguese galleon they were about to attack was storm damaged, but what they didn't know was it had jettisoned every one of its cannons. With no way of fighting off an attack, the marauders quickly took control of the damaged galleon, and began dividing the treasure up. So large was the bounty that the pirate crew received 50,000 golden guineas apiece (which today would be worth almost twelve million dollars). Levasseur and Taylor took even more, and then decided to go their separate ways. Taylor disappeared, no doubt to enjoy his unimaginable wealth, whereas Levasseur settled in the Seychelles. He should've stayed there, but itchy feet sent him to Madagascar where he was captured, tried and sentenced to death by hanging.

According to legend, as Levasseur was standing upon the scaffold, he threw his necklace into the crowd. It contained a coded message. As it disappeared into the mass of people, he yelled, "Find my treasure, ye who may understand it!"

Lavasseur was hanged at precisely 5pm on 7th July 1730, aged just forty. The whereabouts of his treasure remains a mystery, a trove that includes golden goblets, coins, diamonds and a seven-foot cross encrusted with so many jewels that today it would be worth over 150 million dollars alone. Many historians believe the treasure is hidden somewhere in the Seychelles.

"I can't believe they don't sell metal detectors in these shops," I said as I finished my coffee. "Because if they did, I'd buy one right now."

Angela was looking out of the window, staring at the gorgeous blue sky and jungle behind the town. She turned back to me and finished her coffee. "I think it's time to go snorkeling."

6

The bay we chose was astonishing for its beauty, and amazing due to the lack of people. The palm-fringed white beach lay hidden beneath a verdant jungle of coconut trees that spilled out over a nearby road. With the sublime turquoise ocean lapping gently against granite rocks, we felt we'd found the exact location of the *Bounty* adverts. In fact the famous TV advertisements for the chocolate-covered coconut bars had been filmed on the neighbouring island of La Digue, but we only found that out later.

"Oh, wow," said Angela for the hundredth time. "This is amazing!" I nodded like a galoot at the vision of pure paradise before us. It was brochure-perfect: all palm trees, white sand and the most gorgeous ocean imaginable. As soon as we'd donned our snorkels, we were in, submerging ourselves into a warm aquarium of tropical fish.

Stripy zebra fish, multi-coloured parrotfish, and silvery fish that resembled tiny sharks all vied for our attention. But I couldn't help feel a little nervous about swimming in such tropical waters. My mind played out the theme tune to *Jaws* every time I spied a dark shadow. After all, two European holidaymakers had been killed fairly recently by sharks in the tranquil waters of the Seychelles, though admittedly on a different island. But neither of us saw any sharks that afternoon, and after an hour we climbed ashore.

"We're doing that again," said Angela. "I felt like I was in a nature documentary."

7

That evening a bat tried to kill me.

Angela spotted the gang of fruit bats as we walked towards a nearby restaurant. Some were flying overhead like extras in a *Scooby Doo* cartoon, but most were dangling from a tree, feasting on some large green fruit. As we moved directly underneath the tree to observe their cute, furry bat bodies up close, one of them tried to murder me.

Whoooosh!

The sound of something zipping past my ear was terrifying, and it had caught me completely off guard. *Thud* was the sound it made as it landed by my foot. The large piece of half-eaten fruit missed my head by mere centimetres. Angela had already jumped back in shock, but I could only stare at the rock-sized, hard-skinned projectile that could have caved my head in. I looked up to see the miscreant scampering away along a branch towards its pals. It was sniggering at me.

"*Jesus!* I've just survived a bat attack!" I said as I moved away from the tree, keeping a suspicious eye out for further assault. "I could've been killed."

"Stop being a drama queen," answered Angela. "You survived getting your head damp. That's all. Now stop going on about it."

I walked on in silence, wondering what curried bat would taste like.

8

The next morning, we decided to drive to the botanical gardens. As it was a Sunday, the local populace were out and about, most of them wearing their finery as they made their way to church. Up ahead, a little girl aged about six ran into the road. She was far enough in front for me to press my brakes easily. As we slowed down, the girl's mother grabbed her and brought her to the safety of the pavement where she began walloping her across the back of the head. We passed them and arrived at the gardens.

The heat was intense and the humidity hellish, but the singing coming from a nearby church was quite uplifting. The gardens looked lush and well kept, full of rare plants and flowers, but Angela and I were there for the giant tortoises.

"They're ugly bastards," I observed as we watched the fifteen or so giant reptiles lounging about in the sun or bathing in a specially dug channel. A couple of tortoises were ponderously walking about, their elongated necks straining so they could sniff the air.

"Did you know," I said to Angela, "in times gone by, families would buy a baby tortoise whenever a newborn girl was brought into the household."

Angela looked at me. "Here, you mean, in the Seychelles?"

I nodded. "Yeah. The tortoise was brought up as a member of the family. The girl would play with it and the whole family would love it like it was their own."

"That's nice," smiled Angela.

"Yes. But when the girl grew up and got married, the tortoise was slaughtered at the wedding ceremony, and feasted upon."

Just next to the tortoise enclosure was a famous Coco de Mer tree, a world record holder because of the seed it produced. It was the largest in the world.

Weighing up to 17kg, the seed was also known as the Love Nut (incidentally the name of a nightclub in downtown Victoria) because its rounded nut resembled a woman's behind. When settlers had first discovered this coincidence, they picked them left, right and centre, but with each fruit taking up to seven years to mature, stocks were soon depleted. Today, the Coco de Mer tree only exists on Mahe Island in a few protected places.

The tree itself was tall and gangly with a huge set of spiky palm-type leaves sprouting from its top section. About twenty or thirty large green fruit hung just below the branches, looking like a cross between giant coconuts and hard mangos. If the bat from the previous night had got his aim right with one of these, I'd be dead now.

We left the tree and followed the pathway through the tropical foliage. Not far was a man asleep on a bench. His broom was leaning against him. As we watched, a mature lady, also armed with a broom, approached him. Smiling to herself, she manoeuvred her broom into position and prodded Mr Sleepyhead in his love nuts. He awoke with a jolt, eyes wide and hands reaching instinctively below. The woman guffawed and moved on.

9

The next day was our last in the Seychelles, and so we decided to drive across to the other side of the island. Along the way, we negotiated uphill hairpin bends and sheer drops that would have tumbled us into the thick rainforest had we clipped the edge. But in the middle of the island, at the top of the hill, we stopped to admire the view. We could see the pristine beaches down below as well as one edge of Victoria, but mainly all we could see was green. The highlands of the Seychelles were abundant in thick vegetation.

After climbing back into the car, we continued driving until we came to a Tea Factory. We decided to pay it a visit.

"I'm sorry," said the smiling lady who appeared from an office at the side. "There is no tea being made today. But you can walk around and see the machinery if you like. Then afterwards, you can visit the cafe. That is open as usual."

After thanking her, Angela and I entered a large room filled with tea making machinery. After a walk along something called the *Withering Section*, we arrived at a selection of other metal contraptions, and I turned to Angela. "This is boring. Who cares about how they make tea? All I want is to try some of the stuff. Come on, let's find the cafe."

The cafe was small but full of tourists, all with a hankering for tea. The counter was a bit threadbare on provisions, offering no cakes or pastries, but we sat down anyway and ordered some speciality teas. Angela ordered vanilla tea while I opted for cinnamon, and five minutes later we were both supping like pensioners in an English tearoom. "Ooh, this is nice," I croaked. "I do like a nice cup of tea."

Fifteen minutes later, we were back in the car heading down the other side of the island.

10

The west coast of Mahe Island is renowned for its beaches. We decided to infiltrate one of the five-star resorts and plumped for the Constance Ephelia Hotel, a resort so posh that it even boasted its own helipad. Wandering by the front desk like we belonged there, we headed past the bar and out the other side, straight into another piece of paradise.

"Wow!" said Angela again, as we stared at the hallucination before us. But it was no mirage; it was real. The ocean was a blend of beautiful aquamarines and turquoises, and the tiny island opposite was the epitome of a tropical isle, all palm trees, granite outcrops and white sand. We found a sun lounger each, deposited our things and waded straight in. With our snorkels at the ready, we aimed for the small island.

"It's like bath water," said Angela. "It's so warm."

We waded further out, but the gradient got no deeper. We seemed to be paddling along an ocean shelf about a foot and a half deep. Nevertheless, we donned the snorkels and submerged ourselves into the shallows, coming face to face with shimmering fish darting back and forth. Tiny blue fish sparkled in the sunlight and a shoal of larger fish sporting colourful pointed mouths swam in front of me. Near some granite rocks, I spied a hermit crab and a shoal of zebra fish. The undersea vision was simply stunning.

The island was tiny, and Angela and I were the only two people on it. "Maybe the treasure's buried here," I quipped as we walked across the island. "It looks like the sort of place a pirate would bury his pieces of eight." Two minutes later were at the other side, staring out at yet another vision of tropical gorgeousness.

"I think the Seychelles may be the most beautiful place we've ever been," said Angela, gazing out across the ocean. "We're so lucky to be here."

"I know." I stared out across the almost transparent ocean.

11

That evening we sat on our balcony watching the sun fall over the Seychelles. We pondered our trip through the Dark Continent.

Quickly we'd realised that Africa wasn't so much a *Dark Continent* as perhaps a *Colourful Continent*. Colour was everywhere in Africa, from the spice stalls of Marrakech to the fruit and vegetables of a Gambian market. Vibrant colours had hit us on the streets of Swaziland, and we'd been mesmerized by the ocean hues in the Seychelles. But this trip was only the first part of our travels through Africa. In six months' time, we would be back. The next portion of our travels would see us returning to North Africa, initially, beginning in the Land of the Pharaohs. It was country I'd always wanted to visit.

Chapter 8: Land of the Pharaohs

Interesting fact: Pharaoh Pepi II coated his slaves in honey to attract flies away from himself.

When I'd been teaching in the Middle East, one of the girls in my class was from Egypt. Eleven-year-old Yara told me that if she looked out her bedroom window in Cairo, she could see the pyramids. The thought of this intrigued me. To be able to see the only remaining Ancient Wonder of the World from the window of your own house: how great would that be? "Wow!" I'd said to her. "That must be amazing!"

Yara shrugged. "Not really. They're just there."

I was astounded. "What do you mean, they're just there?"

"I don't even notice them. No one does."

I nodded, though not quite believing that something as extraordinary as the Great Pyramids could become so mundane and normal. But perhaps that was what happened if you lived under the shadow of something amazing. Maybe even the Taj Mahal would become boring after a month of living beside it. When Yara went out for break, I promised myself that I would see the pyramids with my own eyes one day.

2

The agenda for our first day in the Egyptian capital was hectic. In the morning, we'd visit the pyramids, and then over lunchtime, we'd wander around the Antiquities Museum. For the afternoon, we'd take a trip to the Citadel of Saladin. A lot to see in one go, but with only two full days in Cairo, we had little time for dallying.

The Sheraton hotel looked plush from the outside and even better from the inside. Porters hurried across the marble-floored lobby whilst businessmen in traditional thawb sat hovering over laptops, all under the gaze of a grand chandelier.

Our room was a bit of a disappointment though. The passage of time hadn't been kind to the curtains and wallpaper. But the view from the balcony made up for this. At whatever time of the day we cared to look down, there was always a bottleneck of traffic at the roundabout below, all beeping, all angry. And in the distance, if we craned our necks to the right, was Tahir Square, the focal point for the 2011 Egyptian Revolution.

3

The morning was warm and hazy. Over breakfast, I said to Angela, "I wonder how long it will be before we're suckered for cash?"

Angela pondered this. After all, we were now fairly experienced travellers. We'd survived the shopkeepers of Marrakech, and did battle with the infamous bumsters of The Gambia. "We'll be fine," said Angela. "We've just got to be firm."

As promised, our driver picked us up at 10am, and we were soon on our way, excited at seeing one of the Wonders of the World. The driver exited the hotel easily enough, but as soon as we hit the main road, insanity caught up with us.

Cairo had, without any doubt, the worst traffic in the world. There was no order to the madness, and the only rule seemed to be: he who beeps loudest is the winner. The gridlock we were in was on the approach to a roundabout. Randomly parked vehicles didn't help matters either, causing logjams behind them. Shrill beeping and angry hand gestures were going on all around us, and I wondered whether there had been a crash.

"No crash," said the driver, a man in his thirties, who was partial to honking his horn at every available opportunity. "Just normal Cairo traffeeck. We will soon be passing the roundabout."

Scam No 1 occurred just a few minutes later. It involved the old papyrus ruse. We were passing rundown shops scrawled with Arabic. Women in headscarves and men in suits wandered past them. As we cleared the roundabout, our driver suddenly spoke up.

"If you like," he said, "I can take you to a special museum. It show you how papyrus is made. Perhaps I take you there now? Is free to enter and it will not take long, maybe thirty minutes?"

From his mirror, I could tell he looked hopeful. Getting a couple of unsuspecting tourists into a papyrus shop would earn him an extra few quid. They'd even give him a drink for his efforts. But unfortunately for him, we'd read up on this very scam just before we'd left the UK.

"No thanks," I said. "Just the pyramids, please." The man nodded and said no more about it.

4

Our driver pointed to the left. Rising over some shops was the top third of a mighty pyramid. Many people believed the pyramids were at the edge of the desert, but we could see for ourselves just how untrue this was.

The driver negotiated a side street with careful skill, eventually arriving at a small square dominated by trinket shops. Dotted around the edge were camels, horses and a couple of donkeys (looking forlorn and depressed, as always).

A man approached the car, and our driver spoke to him in thick Arabic. After a few seconds, the driver turned to address us. "This man will take you around pyramids. His name is Saieed. Please follow him. I wait here."

As we climbed out, a boy leading a flock of goats wandered past. The new man saw me looking and explained a little about them. "These animals are for sale," he told me. "And a good one will cost one thousand Egyptian Pounds (£100). If you want to buy one, just let me know, and I will arrange everything for you."

Saieed led us into a small building that looked like a shop, and told us to sit down. He disappeared, leaving us alone to stare about the place. If it was a shop, it sold mainly perfumes and scented oils because they were all over the room. "Do you think we're in the right place?" I whispered to Angela. "Or is this another scam?"

Before Angela could answer, Saieed reappeared with a tray of tea. After we'd taken a small glass each, he sat down opposite and asked a strange question. "Would you prefer camel or horse?"

I was taken aback, and judging from Angela's expression, she was too. Was Saieed offering us some sort of meat dish or did he think we were in the livestock business?

The man seemed to sense our confusion and grinned. "To travel around the Great Pyramids, you must choose either camel or horse."

Ah, I thought. "Can't we just walk?" I asked.

Saieed shook his head. "You must choose camel or horse."

Angela looked excited. Hedging my bets, I asked Saieed which was more comfortable, and after looking me up and down, he said he'd get two horses.

Two horses? Why would we need two horses for our carriage? Surely we weren't that heavy. But then to my utter dismay it became clear why we'd need two horses. One each. A few minutes later, he led us outside to the waiting nags.

5

As I contemplated riding on a horse for the first time in twenty years, another man arrived with a couple of saddles. Before I knew it, both Angela and I were on our mighty steeds. The lack of helmets or jodhpurs soon became a secondary concern as we trotted off along a dusty street. Just keeping upright on the damn thing was hard enough.

"Follow me," said Saieed, riding adeptly on a horse of his own. "And do not worry, I look after you. And maybe later we make horse go very fast! You will enjoy, I promise!"

While I got used to my horse, Saieed led towards a rear entrance of the pyramid complex. It was well away from the usual tourist arrival point but was still crowded with people, camels, horses and donkeys. As we neared it, we encountered *Scam No 2*, a more elaborate ruse this time. This one involved a headdress tout.

The man with the fold of cloth laid over his arm approached us with a large smile on his bearded face. As he got nearer, he began folding the cloth into an Arab-style headdress. I knew if he got the chance, he'd put it over my head and secure it in place with a strip of rubber. Then he'd demand money. As his arm moved towards me, I waved him away immediately. *Be gone, rapscallion!*

"But it look good for photo!" the man said, attempting to get the thing close to my head. I gave him my best Clint Eastwood stare and rode on, leaving him in the dust from my horse's hooves. Further along, I noticed a family of five, all wearing headdresses. Dad looked glum.

6

Once through the entrance (with no sign yet of the great structures), Saieed handed us over to a large fat man in a long white robe.

"Welcome!" the robed man boomed as he led our horses by their harnesses. Once away from the packed entrance, he stopped and passed me a bottle of Fanta that my hand accepted in reflex. And somehow during the transaction, he'd managed to pop the lid. I immediately became suspicious and told the man I didn't want it. I tried to hand it back, but he refused to accept.

"Is hot day!" he boomed jovially. "Drink! Is good to drink on hot day!" Behind me, I noticed Angela had also been passed a drink and I began to think that maybe they were part of the deal. After all, Saieed was nowhere to be seen, and the man was right, it was hot and I was actually thirsty. Perhaps the tour of the pyramids was going to be with a series of guides: one to get us to the entrance, another to lead us around, and maybe a third to take us back to the car. With the hot sun overhead, I took a slurp of my Fanta just as the fat man wandered over.

"Okay," he said. "You give money now for drinks."

Scam No 3 had been an expert con job. Shaking my head, I couldn't believe we'd fallen into his trap so easily. Reluctantly I gave the man a small amount of change, and he disappeared, on the lookout for more victims, no doubt. Saieed appeared and quickly worked out what had happened.

"Do not listen or speak to anyone except me," he warned. "They will always want money."

"But we thought you handed us over to him," I said.

"No! I go to buy entrance tickets!"

Onwards we trotted into the sands of the Sahara.

7

Despite the rip-off touts, the horse ride around the pyramids was turning out to be great fun. And though I found sitting on a saddle uncomfortable, I still managed to keep upright, even during a speedy canter across the rubble-infested sand. The three Great Pyramids of Giza loomed up over a rise of hills and were every bit as spectacular as we had expected. A few minutes later, we arrived at the base of one of them. It was huge. And bumpy.

From a distance, the pyramids seem smooth and sleek, but up close, they look rough and uneven. None of the slabs appeared the same size, and a fair few had large chips in them that had created a mess of boulders and debris at the bottom. Still, they were the Great Pyramids, and I felt lucky to be so close to them. I wondered whether Saieed felt the same sense of awe.

"No," he admitted. "I do not feel excited by the pyramids anymore. I see them almost every day. But I do enjoy it when tourists see them for the first time. I like to see *their* excitement."

We'd chosen a good time to visit the pyramids because we had the place more or less to ourselves. Most tourists, Saieed told us, arrived either around eight in the morning or else after sunset. Apart from us, there was only one security guard wandering about.

"Climb up if you like," offered Saieed. "The guy over there will not stop you. He is my friend."

We declined and instead snapped off a few photos.

8

As we rode towards the Sphinx, Angela asked Saieed how long he'd been riding.

"About fifteen years," he said. "Half my life. And I can ride any horse. Egyptian, Spanish, even Arabian. A short while ago I told your husband that the pyramids no longer excited me, but if he'd asked what did excite me, I would have told him, horses."

The Sphinx looked so familiar that it was difficult to comprehend that we were seeing it for the first time. Even without its nose it looked remarkable, apparently the largest single-stone statue in the world.

"There are a few reasons why the nose is missing," Saieed said, as we watched a large white coach pull up beside the Great Sphinx of Giza. Tourists spilled out, gawping upwards and firing camera shots at the great thing. Another coach pulled up behind them.

"Some people think it was chiselled off in the fourteenth century by a Muslim cleric, angry at local peasants for making offerings to the Sphinx. Other people think some of Napoleon's soldiers fired cannon balls at it."

Five minutes later, the tourists had finished taking their photos and their umbrella-wielding guide cajoled them back into their air-conditioned coaches. Their tour seemed quick and clean, but certainly not as much fun as riding around by horseback.

Thirty minutes later, Angela and I were back in the square we had started from. As promised, our driver was there waiting for us, a newspaper flopped out over his sleeping face. After a quick nudge from Saieed, he awoke and we said farewell. It was time to visit the great museum.

9

The Egyptian Antiquities Museum was founded in 1835 as a way of curbing the looting of the pyramids. Almost every corner of the vast building was a feast for the eyes: golden chariots, Tutankhamun's famous burial mask, regal-looking thrones and so much more. The whole place reeked of Ancient Egypt, but the layout was haphazard, with seemingly little thought for the placement of artefacts.

Even worse, we discovered, was that many of the displays had no information about them. We could have been staring at the burial shroud of an ancient pharaoh, or maybe the rag from an old palace hag, we simply couldn't tell. Another niggling problem was the lack of signposts. In a building as immense as the Egyptian Museum, we expected a few signs telling us where to go, but as far as we could tell, there were none. For people with a guide this was not a problem, but Angela and I had no choice but to wander aimlessly.

By chance, we came across the Royal Mummy Hall. For 100 Egyptian Pounds each (£10) we were allowed access to a small room filled with actual mummies. The room was packed to capacity, everyone stooping and staring at the twelve grisly bodies.

Some of the mummies looked like something out of a horror film, about to come alive and stalk the corridors in search of meat. All had age-darkened faces, and bodies covered from the neck downwards in some sort of burial shroud. Some had withered arms crossed over their chests, their hands covered in bandages. We walked around the macabre room, eyeing the gruesome remains of former pharaohs. It was easily the best part of the museum.

"Right," I said as we left the room. "That's the museum done. Only the citadel left. Come on."

10

The Citadel of Saladin, located in the old part of Cairo, dates from the 12th century. At that time, it consisted of walls, watchtowers and gates, but in the 19th century, someone decided to add the Mohammed Ali Mosque. Angela and I stood beneath the great beige structure. It looked like it belonged in Istanbul.

Two of its minarets were huge, towering high above the multi-domed roof. After removing our shoes, we entered the cavernous interior, stepping on the massive carpet littered with people, either praying or sitting in circles with their tour guides. The best bit was the gigantic dangling chandelier in the middle. A mesmerising number of lights made it dance and sparkle before our eyes.

Back outside, the views from the citadel walls were equally impressive. They highlighted a horizon of mosques and ancient buildings. By squinting our eyes, we could obscure the skyscrapers in the background, which made the vision look almost Biblical. Every building was sandstone coloured and *old*. As if on cue, the Muslim call to prayer began, and for a brief moment, Cairo was truly magical.

11

The next morning, we jumped in one of Cairo's most common features – the black-and-white taxi. The one we chose, like the vast majority of them, was a small elderly Fiat that had seen better days. The dashboard was basic, but had the bonus of a bunch of loose wires. Some sort of ancient meter, which clearly hadn't worked for at least a decade, hung just below the dash, and the name emblazoned upon it summed things up nicely: *Hovel*.

Inside, the scent of petrol hung in the air, and we were not surprised at the absence of seatbelts. Our driver, a middle-aged man wearing a faded grey suit, got in and started the engine. With a grinding of gears, we were off, blazing into the chaos of Cairo's traffic system.

The driver was one of those special breeds who liked nothing better than shouting, swearing and raising his fist at any driver foolish enough to get in his way. He seemed to get particularly angry with pedestrians. Guttural Arabic was yelled to any man, woman or child who dared cross his path. And there were plenty who did. Some were small children, but the man cared not a jot. The taxi driver was also a master swerver. It was as thrilling as being on a waltzer when he veered past people crossing in front of him, especially when he did it one-handed so he could shake his fist.

Ten minutes later, we were dropped off outside the Grand Hyatt.

12

On the fortieth floor of the Grand Hyatt was a revolving restaurant. Being midday meant the restaurant was closed, but thankfully the bar was open.

"This is great," I said. "Just look at the view of the Nile!"

It was a potent river, spanned by a series of vehicle-clogged bridges. Small boats were making their way along the Nile, and beyond the banks on both sides of the river, jetties and skyscrapers battled for space. Further back, behind the grime of Cairo, and half-obscured by haze, we could see the pyramids. We ordered some drinks, and for the next thirty minutes, we enjoyed views spanning the whole city, even if we weren't revolving.

Instead of catching a taxi to our hotel, we decided to walk. From our vantage point in the Hyatt, we had located our hotel and quickly worked out a simple way of getting back to it. Little did we realise that the route would be filled with *Leer People*.

Leer People were men aged thirteen and upwards. They loitered outside shops, or stood against walls. Sometimes they were on passing buses, or sat slumped in the back of taxis. Some of them were the taxi drivers themselves, but they all had one thing in common, they *leered*.

Some men looked at Angela with such lustful leers that it became quite scary. Groups of teenage boys would leer at her with undisguised glee, looking her up and down with lascivious grins. And in the traffic jam spanning the bridge over the Nile, virtually every man leered with obvious interest.

At the other side of the bridge, we came to a small three-windowed booth. It contained the *King of the Leermen*. His Royal Highness was a traffic policeman. Spying our approach, the fat officer shifted position so he could leer at Angela with full undisguised joy. His attention was so focussed that I reckoned I could've sneaked up and banged him on the head. As we passed the front of his booth, he shifted his gaze. His look was full of lust, and it was a good job I could only see him from the waist upwards. As we passed the booth, the randy copper made use of his third window. Behind him, the traffic beeped and fumed, but he couldn't have cared less.

13

Later that afternoon we took a felucca along the Nile. The cushions on the deck of the craft were a bit strange, looking like they had been looted from a childcare centre. They were bright yellow, and featured cartoons of rabbits. The man in charge was a skilled mariner, however, manipulating the single sail (emblazoned with *Vodaphone,* for some reason) with precision and skill. We headed out into the middle of the Nile and sat back as a pleasing breeze began to cool our faces.

"This is the only way to travel in Cairo," I said to Angela, who was sunning herself at the back of the felucca. "No traffic fumes and mad beeping. Just the wind in our hair, and the sound of gently-lapping water."

With a slight turn of the tiller, the captain manoeuvred us away from another boat coming in the opposite direction. A cigarette dangled from one hand, a fixture of most men in the Egyptian capital we'd noticed. We sat back, enjoying the journey. It was a nice way to end our brief stopover in Cairo.

14

That night, we caught a taxi back to the airport. The driver was the same man who had taken us to the Hyatt the day before, because we'd already booked him. So dilapidated was his taxi that at first the security guards would not allow him to enter the hotel grounds. It was only after some furious waving on our part that they finally relented.

As he trundled up in his banger, other official hotel taxi drivers began to laugh. Then they stared at us, obviously wondering why we'd chosen such a decrepit mode of transport instead of their limousines. As our man stepped out, still in the same grey suit, a hotel porter clapped him on the back, as if to say, how did you manage to secure this fare? Feeling slightly self-conscious, we climbed into the cramped Fiat and set off.

The forty-minute journey to the airport was as thrilling as being on a roller coaster. Without seatbelts, we were tossed this way and that, as the madman jerked his car around to avoid collision after collision. There was a fair amount of shake fisting and yelling too, which only added to the excitement, and when it started raining, the adrenalin rush was notched up another step.

For a start, his windscreen wipers didn't work, even after some furious yelling and windscreen banging. Driving with a rain-filled windscreen looked a tricky proposition, but the man coped well, moving his head from side to side like a demented meercat. Somehow we arrived outside the airport terminal, safe and sound.

As Angela released her grip on the seats, she let out a sigh of relief. But then we hit the final snag of the journey: neither of the back doors would open. The driver was frantically pulling on Angela's door to remedy this.

"Because of rain!" he yelled through a tiny gap in the window. Angela and I glanced at each other, wondering whether to start laughing or crying. The taxi driver huffed, puffed, and pulled even more. We sat back, trapped in his taxi, contemplating our fate. But then the man came up with another plan of attack and came around to my side of the car, and yanked hard. It worked.

We were free to catch our flight to Ethiopia.

Chapter 9: Onwards to Addis Ababa

Interesting fact: Ethiopia is the only African country with its own alphabet.

Addis Ababa was not what we expected.

Before arriving in the Ethiopian capital, Angela and I had visions of a full-blown Third World city: beggars dressed in rags, tin-roofed shacks, and stick-like people covered in dust and flies.

But it wasn't like that at all. For a start, the vast majority of people on the streets of Addis Ababa were well dressed, and quite a large proportion of them wore western-style clothing. Sure, plenty of people looked thin, but not unhealthily so. There were also lots of shops, and even a few small malls to cater for the upwardly mobile of the city. A fair proportion of the vehicles on the road had seen better days, but they certainly were not the dilapidated wrecks we'd anticipated seeing.

There was construction work going on all over the city too, which, judging by the placards outside the building works, suggested that Addis Ababa was a city on the up and up. In a few years' time, it would have an impressive set of skyscrapers.

That said, there were enough reminders to tell us we were not in New York or Hong Kong. For a start, the smog was bad, mostly coming from the cars and trucks clogging up the streets. And above our heads circled vultures and kites, searching out scraps of carrion. And then there were the homeless people, quite often lying comatose by the side of streets, wrapped in dusty old clothes, and being sniffed at by feral dogs.

Pot-holed pavements were another indicator that we were not in Paris or Dubai, with some of them so large and deep that life-threatening injuries would almost certainly result if a person fell into one. Furthermore, instead of FedEx delivery trucks, people carted stuff about on their heads, or else on the back of donkeys or oxen. Yes, we were indeed in Africa, though not quite the one we had imagined.

2

Despite being one of the most successful and profitable airlines of Africa, Ethiopian Airlines still received calls from worried Westerners, inquiring whether food would be served aboard their flights. Well our food was fine, as was the wine. The modern Boeing 737 delivered us into Bole International Airport at around 8am, local time.

After obtaining visas from a poky-looking side room, Angela and I were ushered to the front of a queue usually reserved for diplomats and aircrew. Why the airport authorities had allowed us to bypass the long line of locals waiting at the other booths, we didn't know, but after only a few minutes' wait, we were stamped into the Federal Democratic Republic of Ethiopia.

Our hotel was only five minutes away from the airport, located in an area full of construction. From our balcony we had a good view of the surrounding city, as well as the shell of a building opposite covered in wooden scaffolding. Beyond the building work, dusty tracks led into waste ground, but at least there was plenty of greenery dotting the landscape. In fact, it was surprising just how green Addis Ababa looked.

"I can't believe we're in Ethiopia," I said, searching out the guidebook. "This is one country I never thought we'd get to."

Angela nodded and then yawned. Neither of us had got much sleep since leaving Cairo.

3

When we told people of our travel plans back home, most had nodded in appreciation when we said we were going to Cairo, and some looked downright jealous at the mention of Zanzibar. A few looked quizzical when we explained about Zambia and Botswana, but almost everyone scrunched their faces when we told them about Ethiopia.

And who could blame them? For a long time in the 1980s, Ethiopia was a major news story. Between 1983 and 1985, the starving of Ethiopia became a daily fixture on television sets across the UK. Harrowing footage depicted a famine that would eventually kill over a million people. As a result, the country became synonymous with poverty and pestilence, an image most Westerners retain to this day, despite the fact that Ethiopia has the highest GDP in East Africa, and one of the fastest-growing economies in the world.

It took some serious persuasion to get Angela to agree to go to Ethiopia. But in the end, it was a simple matter of logistics. The cheapest flight from Cairo to Zanzibar was with Ethiopian Airlines, and since it involved stopping in Addis Ababa to change planes, why not add it to the itinerary? The chance to visit Ethiopia, I pointed out, might never come around again. Luckily, Angela agreed with my reasoning.

4

Tomoca Cafe was a popular place in Addis Ababa. The strong aroma of coffee hit us as soon as we stepped in, but we weren't the only Westerners there. A tour group had arrived just before us and more or less filled the place. They sounded American, and we could have been in downtown Seattle, not sub-Saharan Africa.

Behind the large counter was an array of coffee beans and coffee-making equipment. After some deliberation, we chose our beverages and the man got to work. A few minutes later, we found a space to stand with our newly-prepared drinks. I took my first sip of the hot black liquid.

"Well?" asked Angela.

"Yeah, it's all right." Although I enjoyed a nice cup of coffee, I was never going to be a connoisseur. To me, one cup of coffee tasted much like the next one. "But at least it should wake me up a bit."

Angela took a sip and then smiled. "This is better than all right. This is *good* coffee. I'm going to buy some to take with us. You're a heathen."

We left the cafe and decided to make our way down Churchill Avenue, a long stretch of road composed of shops, cafes, bus stops and people sitting around doing nothing in particular. Low-level telephone wires and corrugated metal roofing gave the scene a distinctly African flavour. The weather was perfect though, an uplifting 23 degrees Celsius (which it was more or less all year round), just warm enough for T-shirts.

"I'll tell you what I've noticed," I said as we ambled along. "I'm getting short of breath a bit here." I was referring to the fact that Addis Ababa was located at an altitude of about 7500ft, making it the fourth-highest capital city in the world. The lack of oxygen in the air meant our lungs were working overtime.

"It'll be good for us," said Angela, sidestepping a cavernous gap in the pavement. "A bit of exercise."

We continued walking, taking in the sights of downtown Addis Ababa. "Uh oh," I said a minute later, spying the man walking towards us. "Here we go…"

5

"Hello! How are you both?" said the young Ethiopian man. Like many of his compatriots, he was a tall, wiry individual with close-cropped hair. "My name is Job – a Biblical name as I'm sure you know – and I am wondering what you are doing here in Addis Ababa?"

Job looked to be in his mid-twenties and seemed friendly enough. His English was good, and he didn't seem to have any concealed weapons about his person. Nevertheless, his presence still put us on guard, so despite his apparent pleasantness, Angela and I brushed him off. We continued along Churchill Avenue.

Job, of course, followed us.

"So are you here as tourists, or perhaps for business? And by the way, I can't help but notice that you, sir, look like an American film star. Perhaps you are one? Am I wrong?"

I smiled and walked on. By my side, Angela said nothing; clearly feeling the same mixture of annoyance and unease. The last thing we needed was someone trailing us around Addis. I wondered how persistent he would be.

While Job chatted about football and other such trivial matters, we passed a large roundabout with a big cannon as its centrepiece. After negotiating an assortment of beggars, traders and shysters (as Angela so eloquently put it), we arrived at a point in the road where we needed to stop to get our bearings. Job stopped too, trying to look over my shoulder at the map.

"Perhaps you would like me to show you where you are?" he said. "I can point on the map?"

"Look," I said, finally acknowledging Job's presence. "Are you going to follow us all day, or have you got anything else to do?"

Job's smile disappeared, replaced with a look of confusion.

"Because we are fine by ourselves," I added. "We don't need you to look after us."

Job nodded and looked deflated. "I understand. I will go now. And I'm sorry to have made you feel uncomfortable." With that he turned on his heels and blended in with the crowd heading south on Churchill Avenue.

I looked at Angela. I felt like a cad of the highest order. It seemed Job hadn't been a shyster after all. He'd been an educated young man only wanting to help us. And now, because of our boorish behaviour, he would remember us as ignorant and ill-mannered Western buffoons, the type of people to avoid or even scowl at in the future.

Angela looked pained. "How horrible are we?"

6

Once we'd established where we were, we continued along Churchill Avenue but the shops weren't particularly interesting, and so we headed back up the hill to the hotel. Instead of going in, however, we decided to go for another wander.

I was pleased to discover that lots of roads and streets in Addis Ababa were named after African countries: Gambia Street, Sudan Street and Zambia Street were just some of them, as was the Democratic Republic of Congo Street. Our hotel was nestled between Cameroon Street, Zimbabwe Street and Cape Verde Street.

Nobody bothered us as we walked along, nimbly sidestepping the potholes and cracks. The locals seemed used to tourists, we felt, not looking in our direction at all.

Half way along the road, we passed a grand-looking church, known as the Bole Medhane Alem Cathedral. Its three aquamarine domes rose majestically above the grime of the city.

"I think I quite like Addis Ababa," said Angela as we turned around, back towards the hotel. We really needed to catch up on some sleep. A small blue taxi pulled up alongside the kerb, but a swift shake of my head soon had him moving off again. In the distance, poking above a line of storefronts, were a few blue-glassed skyscrapers. The early-morning smog was slowly disappearing. I nodded in agreement. Addis looked just fine.

7

The next day Gabriel, a 30-year-old tour guide, picked us up for a morning of sightseeing. He spoke excellent English and wasted no time in leading us to the car and driver.

"Is this your first time in Ethiopia?" he asked.

Angela answered him. "Yes."

Gabriel smiled. "Well, I hope it will not be your last."

He told us that the first place we would visit was the Ethiopian National Museum, the home of Lucy.

Lucy was the skeleton of a hominid woman who was 3.2 million years old. Her discovery in 1974 caused ripples of archaeological excitement because her remains, unlike other finds, were still intact. It meant scientists could study this early ancestor of man like they had never done before.

The outside of the museum looked like a typical 1960s concrete office block. Without the lush palm trees and darting lizards, we could have been in the middle of a UK town centre. The three of us climbed some steps and entered the building.

8

Had it not been for Gabriel, Angela and I might have walked right past the pile of old bones inside the glass cabinet. Lucy's room was neither signposted nor especially well lit. Plus it was little more than a broom cupboard. Whoever designed the exhibit needed to have a major rethink.

The bones were actually replicas of the ones found in the seventies, with the real bones locked safe inside the museum vaults. Next to the bones was a mock-up of what the woman's skeleton would have looked like. I couldn't get over how small she was, little more than the size of a child.

As well as Lucy, the museum contained the usual assortment of pots, weapons, tools and clothing – the same sort of stuff found in museums all over the world. Left to our own devices, we'd have finished the whole lot in about ten minutes, but with Gabriel following us, we felt obliged to stare at the offerings for longer than usual. "Hmmm, this is an interesting bit of pot," I whispered to Angela. "And there are so many more bits like this in here."

I was bored to hell, and couldn't help stifle a yawn. Angela was bored too, and so we tried to move around the exhibits at a slightly nippier pace.

"Hold on!" said Gabriel, "You've missed this out. And it is interesting because...." And so we slowed down to look at the pot in question.

9

"Tell me," asked Gabriel an hour later, as we began the ten-kilometre drive to Entoto Hill, a place where he promised we would get a good view of Addis Ababa. "What are the houses like in England?"

I thought for a moment before answering. "Some are big and some are small."

Gabriel nodded and asked whether any of the houses in England were like the ones we could see outside now. The dwellings we were passing were mostly simple shacks with metal roofs attached in the most rudimentary of fashions. Some of them had satellite dishes attached though. I had to concede that the houses in England were not like them, and told Gabriel this.

Gabriel looked pensive for a second or two. "Then I think perhaps I would like to live in England."

I nodded but told him that it was usually cold and windy, and often raining too. "Plus it's really expensive," I added.

"I understand all of that, but I think the overall quality of life is better in England than it is here in Ethiopia."

I had to agree.

10

We began a drive up a steep curving hill populated by donkeys, goat herders, and women carrying backbreaking amounts of firewood on their backs. Gabriel informed us that the women did the trip twice a day, to sell what they had collected for a few birr (the Ethiopian currency). I looked at one woman and couldn't believe the amount of wood tied to her back. God help her if she ever fell over, I thought, because she'd never be able to get up again.

"Why don't men carry wood?" asked Angela.

Gabriel smiled. "In Ethiopia, carrying these bundles is seen as women's work. Even if a man has no job, he will not carry the wood. He would rather sit on his porch all day and do nothing."

At the top of the hill was a church painted in red, green and yellow, the same colours as the Ethiopian flag. As well as its interesting exterior, the church offered a good lookout point. We made our way up to a small platform where we could see the sprawl of Addis Ababa below us, home to around four million people. With its backdrop of mountains, and with numerous kites riding the thermals, Addis looked African. After snapping a few photos, we all walked along a stony path towards the former Palace of Emperor Menelik.

"Emperor Menelik reigned between 1889 and 1913," said Gabriel, "He was the final Ethiopian monarch to have a direct male link to King Solomon and the Queen of Sheba."

To be honest, I'd always thought that the Queen of Sheba was a made-up person, but Gabriel explained that she was a monarch whose kingdom had probably been in Ethiopia, or maybe Yemen. We followed Gabriel around a slight bend, and came face to face with our first Ethiopian palace.

It was a collection of large thatched huts, next to a tall tree with two squawking vultures perched in its branches. A young boy with two goats eyed us as we passed him.

"Menelik founded the first bank in Ethiopia," Gabriel said. "And started the first postal system. Also, according to one story I have heard, Menelik had an electric chair."

"An electric chair?" I said, shocked. "As in the ones that kill people?"

Gabriel sniggered. "Yes, the same ones that kill people. When he found out about America using them to execute criminals, he ordered three for himself. When they arrived in Addis Ababa, he was excited, but then realised they would not work. Back then, Ethiopia had no electricity to power the chairs. Instead he had one installed as his throne. Come, let's go inside."

There was nothing, not even an exhibit or a picture, inside the hut. The room we were standing in consisted of a bare wooden floor with a curved, white-plastered wall. Gabriel led us through other similar rooms, including one that had been a large gathering hall.

"That is where the Emperor and his wife sat during important banquets," he explained. "And where the food was served."

I tried to picture the emperor eating his lunch while sitting on a throne made from an electric chair. What a sight that would have been.

We went back outside. The vultures were still squawking, and the boy with the goats was still there. There was also an old man wearing a faded green uniform and cap. He was standing near a large flagpole. Gabriel told us he was the palace security guard. We stood enjoying the clean mountain air for few moments. Then it was time to head back down the hill.

11

Merkato Market claimed to be the largest open-air market in Africa.

"Today is Saturday," Gabriel explained. "So it is the busiest day for trading. That means many people are here, and some of them are dishonest. There is a high chance one of them will try to pickpocket you. For that reason – and if it is agreeable with you – we won't stop in Merkato, but will drive through it slowly so you can get a taste of what is on offer."

We thought this sounded like a good idea.

According to the Lonely Planet, it was possible to buy camels and automatic weapons in Merkato Market, though Angela and I saw no evidence of this. The majority of stalls seemed to be flogging clothes and shoes.

Donkeys wandered along with their backs piled high with goods. Tiny blue and white taxis were parked at intersections; their drivers stood chatting to one another. Everywhere, people were rummaging for the best bargains, or else pushing carts filled with khat.

Khat is a slow-growing shrub endemic to East Africa and Arabia. The chewing of its leaves is popular because of the mild stimulant they offer. Legal in much of the Horn of Africa, we'd seen plenty of men chewing the stuff, but the market seemed the centre of khat. Bundles of it lay in baskets tied with string.

After driving around another similar line of jumbled stalls, we drove back to the hotel. We said good-bye to Gabriel and headed inside.

12

So what did we make of Addis Ababa?

Quite a lot, actually. Angela managed to sum it up well. "The people are friendly, the prices are cheap, and the countryside is breath-taking. I mean, when we went up that mountain road, I could've stayed there for hours, just watching everyone going about their daily business."

"And, compared to the traffic of Cairo," I said, "Addis Ababa is sedate. I reckon even I could drive here."

The Ethiopian capital *had* surprised us, that much was clear. Although we couldn't imagine tourists ever flocking to the city, we both agreed that it could be a nice little stopover, especially with Bole Airport being such an East African hub. We packed our bags in preparation for the next segment of our trip: Zanzibar, the Spice Islands. Both of us were looking forward to some sun and sand in our second Indian Ocean paradise.

Chapter 10: Spice Island

Interesting fact: The shortest war in history was between the United Kingdom and Zanzibar. It took 38 minutes for the Sultan of Zanzibar to surrender.

Just the name, *Zanzibar*, sounds exotic. It rolls off the tongue and conjures visions of white sand, palm trees and clear blue oceans. What it doesn't invoke are images of marauding bandits with machetes. But in 2001, that's exactly what Zanzibar was like.

Zanzibar lies off the coast of Tanzania, and, following some national elections in the mother country (Tanzania), Zanzibar became a centre of violence. Rioters battled with the authorities in the narrow streets of Stone Town, setting cars alight and torching bars. The police responded by firing teargas at the mobs. Things escalated when a policeman's body was found. He'd been decapitated. By the time the bloodshed had ended, thirty-one people were dead.

More than a decade later, the British Foreign Office was offering fresh warnings. They advised UK nationals to avoid Tanzania (and specifically Zanzibar) due to elections being held at the end of the month. After a brief search on the Internet, I discovered that elections were held every four years in Tanzania and that, historically, scenes of mass unrest followed them. Our proposed arrival would be a few days after these elections. We could be heading into a machete war zone.

"What do you think?" I asked Angela before we had even set off on our second trip to Africa. With Zanzibar being such a potential hotspot, we had to think carefully.

"I'm not sure…?"

I thought that maybe it would be wise to scrap Zanzibar from the list, but that would mean getting rid of Addis Ababa too. "No, I'm not sure either."

"Were tourists ever caught up in the violence that happened before?" asked Angela.

"I don't think so…"

"So we might be all right then."

"…or we might not be."

In the end, we decided to go ahead with our plans, and were glad we did. The elections ran smoothly, so the chance of being hacked to death after an afternoon spent napping by the pool was slim.

2

Zanzibar Airport's immigration building was little more than a single structure containing a security booth, some moneychangers, and a bench for luggage to be deposited on. After paying fifty dollars each for a visa, we were soon on our way to the hotel, located on the other side of the island.

After bypassing the edge of Zanzibar City, we entered the lush greenery of the interior. Palm trees were everywhere, as were smaller plants with huge leathery leaves; they gave the place a suitably tropical feel. It reminded us a bit of the Seychelles, only without the hills and granite. And even though Zanzibar was associated with sun, the weather was actually slightly overcast, and even a bit drizzly. We didn't care, it still looked great.

The main road was okay, but the tracks leading away from it were dusty (and now muddy) pathways. Children played in the doorways of some dwellings, amid chickens pecking in the earth. Some of the homes were traditional thatched-roof types, but others were little more than breezeblock shacks with metal corrugated roofing. On virtually every building was a poster of one of the candidates from the recent election.

The traffic was light, consisting of mainly pedestrians, men on bicycles, and the occasional cart being pulled by single oxen. Even so, our passage was not as swift as expected, due to the potholes and puddles. Angela and I had no choice but to sit back and enjoy the landscape of an island once home to slave traders and spice merchants.

3

The name Zanzibar actually came from the Arabic term, *Land of the Black Men,* named so by Omani Arabs who had taken over the island from the Portuguese in the 17th century. A succession of sultans had then ruled Zanzibar, until the British came in the late 19th century. Most of the Arabs had long since gone, leaving behind a mainly Swahili African population.

"Hotel is very close," said the driver as he negotiated his way past a wobbly man on a bicycle.

We looked ahead and waited for it to appear, which it did a few minutes later. Built amid a forest of lush green, the hotel was a massive building with a gigantic thatched roof. The ocean was just behind it, and Angela and I looked at each other and smiled. We were going to like Zanzibar.

The hotel catered mainly for Italian tourists, we found out, with signs written in Italian everywhere. After checking in, a wiry fellow dressed as a Massai warrior led us to our beach bungalow. Breaking the illusion slightly were the hands-free headphones wrapped around his ear, but at least he had a spear and a colourful red shawl.

The room came with a large mosquito net around the bed, and a balcony view towards the Indian Ocean. Even under the grey layer of cloud, the beach looked amazing. We were eager to see how it was going to compare to the Seychelles.

Half an hour later, the weather had cleared, as it frequently did in the tropics, and Angela and I were on the beach. It was the beach of most people's dreams. It seemed to stretch for miles, the palm trees and wooden boats offering a view normally seen in high-end holiday brochures. It didn't have the granite rocks of the

Seychelles, but it did have nicer sand. It was the whitest we'd ever seen, almost flour-like in appearance.

"Ciao!" said a local man, sidling alongside us. They were a few of them on the beach, mostly sat with little blankets of trinkets, or else waiting at juice stands. The man obviously thought we were Italians because he began speaking in the language of Rome. Not that we understood any of it. After realising we were not from Italy, the man switched to decent English.

"How long have you been in Zanzibar? And what are your plans? How about I show you my little shop?"

After the bumsters of The Gambia, this man was a novice. After telling him that we might visit his shop later, he smiled graciously, and pointed to where it was. It was a small shack at the edge of the beach, under the shade of some palm trees. His was one of many.

Later, when another man approached, I decided to pretend I was Russian in an attempt to thwart any conversion. Laying on my thickest KGB accent, I told him I was from Moscow, and had been to Zanzibar many times previously. The man nodded, but carried on harassing us as we walked upon the white powdery sand. In the end, I managed to keep up my Russian accent for about ten minutes until he grew bored and wandered off in search of other white faces.

4

"I think I've been bitten," I said the next morning, scratching and then examining the itchy spot on my leg.

"Do you know what," replied Angela. "So have I."

We regarded the mosquito net, checking for gaps or holes but couldn't find any. So how had the little bastard entered, we wondered? And then I heard the unmistakable sound of a buzz past my ear. I batted at it but made no contact with the bloodsucker.

"It's in here!" I said, whipping my head sideways to spot the blighter. "It's been trapped in all night! Bloody mosquito net!"

"Good job we've been taking our malaria tablets."

After breakfast, we passed under a long wooden jetty. It stuck out into the sea with a thatched building at the far end. It was the epitome of a beach utopia. Helping matters was the sun. Unlike the previous day, it was out on full force, but the temperatures were pleasantly hot rather than overbearing. Just beyond the jetty were some small dhows with Arabian-type sails bobbing around.

"I can't get over this sand," said Angela.

I stooped to pick some up. "If we bagged it up in clear plastic bags, airport security would definitely get their rubber gloves out."

Local children riding bicycles, or ambling in small groups, often approached, speaking Italian at first until switching to broken English. One group of giggling teenage girls made a bold approach for us, but then swerved away at the last second. All of them were laughing nervously. One of the girls was carrying a Bible. Later, two small girls, aged perhaps four, approached.

"Dollar or Euro! Dollar or Euro!" they cried, but only half-heartedly. One of them stepped between us and took Angela's hand, and then mine. Impudently she mimed that she wanted us to swing her. This we did, and afterwards her friend wanted a go too.

Compared to the natural beauty of the beaches in Seychelles, Zanzibar came second. But with its friendly locals and smiling children, Zanzibar easily won.

5

"A bottle of Kilimanjaro beer please," I said to the young woman working behind the counter of the small open-air beach bar. She nodded and went to the fridge. After placing the bottle on the bar in front of me, she asked for thirty thousand shillings. I fished in my wallet and handed it over, thinking that thirty thousand seemed a bit steep. Luckily I had a small conversion table in my wallet.

Thirty thousand shillings was twelve bloody quid! Without touching the bottle, I shouted the woman over and told her I wasn't going to pay that much for one bottle of beer. She nodded, and handed me back twenty-five thousand shillings without comment.

"Why do they do that sort of thing?" Angela said as we sat down. "If she'd charged a reasonable amount, then we would've come back here. But not now. She's burned her bridges. We're not going to trust anyone on this beach now, are we? None of the shopkeepers, none of the men selling boat tours, none of the women selling necklaces. But thank God you realised how much you were being charged."

"Shysters," I said, once again using my new favourite word in the world. "Bloody shysters."

6

The next morning we hired a taxi to take us to Zanzibar City, the busy portside town on the western side of the Island. Even though Zanzibar was part of Tanzania, it had its own government and capital city.

Zanzibar City had a population of around two hundred thousand, and consisted of two sections: Stone Town and Ng'ambo, which literally meant 'The Other Side.' Stone Town was the old part of the city where all the tourists went, and in 2000, UNESCO had declared it a World Heritage Site. We were eager to see it.

A torrential downpour that had started just prior to our arrival was covering the cobbles and pathways in brown puddles. We clambered out of the taxi and ran straight for the nearest shop. Other tourists had done the same thing, and all of us began browsing the wooden carvings and African masks. Finally, with a respite in the rain, Angela and I headed back outside, mindful of the small motorcycles zipping around trying to splash us.

Our guidebook stated that Stone Town contained unique architecture, fusing elements from Africa, Arabia, Europe and Asia. And it was correct. Arches, minarets, and colonial buildings vied for position in Stone Town. Local women wearing brightly coloured wraps wandered the alleyways that crisscrossed it. We might have been in the tourist centre of Zanzibar, but it was still a town made up mainly of local people.

We strolled towards the harbour, a part of the town renowned for its touts and shysters. True to form, a few dodgy-looking Zanzibastards approached us, but they were easy to shake off, helped no doubt by the heavy numbers of other tourists they could bother.

Many buildings along the harbour front had clearly seen better days. Some were in need of a damned good clean. One building that looked okay though was Beit-el-Ajaib, or House of Wonders, one of the largest buildings on the island. In its prime, in the late 1890s, an Omani sultan had used it as a ceremonial palace. Back then, it would have looked magnificent, with marble columns, a tall clock tower, and a menagerie of chained-up wild animals on the front lawn. The sultan had made the front door large enough for his elephant to fit through.

Angela and I stared up at the huge white building, which was now a museum. Three storeys high, it still possessed its clock tower, but instead of chained-up lions, the building had a bench and a set of palm trees.

7

In the 19th century, Omanis had traded African slaves by the boatload. Men, women and children from mainland Africa were captured, and then packed aboard dhows bound for Zanzibar. By the time they reached the harbour of Stone Town, many were starving and weak. Those deemed incapable of fetching a good price at the slave market were killed and thrown overboard.

Nowadays, an Anglican cathedral stands on the site of the old slave market. It was a large building, which had probably been beige at one point, but was now a dirty black colour. Streaks of grime were embedded into its exterior walls. Inside the cathedral, its high altar marked the position of the old whipping post.

Nearby was a hostel with an interesting basement. Preserved underneath the hostel were a couple of slave cells, which, for a small fee, could be visited. Angela and I climbed down a set of stone steps into a dimly-lit and low-ceilinged cellar. The cells looked awful, all concrete walls and columns, with tiny slits for window.

A small group of people were already down in the cellar, listening to a bound and shackled man (in the original chains), speaking of the conditions for the slaves.

"This cell," he said, referring to the low-ceilinged concrete room he was crouching in, "was where slaves were imprisoned for days at a time. They had little air, and no food or toilets. Arab traders would eventually lead the slaves outside to the whipping post, in order of size. Large men who did not pass out would always fetch the highest price at market."

There was a slave monument outside. In a concrete-lined pit stood five life-sized stone statues, metal chains attached to rings around their necks. The expression on their faces was sombre, as if they had accepted their fate, but only with extreme sorrow. A nearby sign read: *The world's last open slave market and notorious place.*

Two small children noticed us looking and approached, giggling. Wearing identical school uniform, and possessing similar facial features, we took them to be brother and sister. We said hello, but they only giggled more, staring into the pit and then at us. I wondered whether they knew what the monument represented.

Stone Town is also famous for its wooden doors. Along the labyrinth of alleyways, intricately carved doors, often covered in metal studs, were a pleasurable distraction for us. Some of the doors were older than the buildings they fronted, and the studs were a tradition brought over from India. They were a deterrent to elephants from charging at them.

Suddenly the heavens opened again, unleashing a torrent of fat raindrops that soaked us before we could do anything. We sought refuge under a shop's awning, but the damage had been done. We waited for a taxi as the puddles began to form again.

8

The next day was another lazy period spent relaxing by the pool and beach. The sun was out, and I could easily see why people would want to come to Zanzibar on holiday. It was just so relaxing. And if people got bored with lazing around, then there were colourful yellow-headed geckos to stare at. It really was an idyllic place to unwind and reset the gears. And with that done, we were almost ready for the next part of our African Adventure. Zambia!

Chapter 11: Livingstone

Interesting fact: Zambia has 1.6 million orphans.

"My friend was driving not far from here," said the taxi driver, as we headed to our hotel from Livingstone Airport. "It was late at night, and he was going too quickly. He did not know there was an elephant in the road ahead of him. By the time he realised, it was too late. He crashed into it."

Angela and I made suitable sounds of shock at the thought of such a thing happening.

The driver continued. "A hurt elephant is the worst kind of elephant. Before my friend could escape the car, the elephant was above him, smashing the roof down with its thick legs. *Crash, crash, crash,* like a potato masher. My friend somehow got out. The elephant disappeared into the forest, and left my friend's car destroyed."

2

From Zanzibar, we had routed southwest to Johannesburg, and, from there, it had been a quick one and a half hour flight to Livingstone – the gateway to Victoria Falls. For our five-night stay, Angela and I shelled out a prince's sum to stay in one of the luxurious riverfront hotels along the mighty Zambezi River. Every room overlooked the river, and signs ominously warned people not to swim in it because of crocodiles, hippos and snakes. We couldn't help but be impressed.

"Look!" said Angela as she gazed out over the balcony towards the river. I joined her and took in the scene – it was one of pure Africa. The river was wide and fast flowing, and just beyond it were the jungles of Zimbabwe, the country that shared Victoria Falls with Zambia.

"And listen to the noises," she added. Exotic birdcalls and chirping insects made it sound as if we were in a nature documentary. We had chosen well, we agreed; the lodge was everything we'd hoped for, even if it was the most expensive hotel we had ever stayed in.

3

The taxi into Livingstone Town took us through dirt tracks lined by scrubland and bush. When we hit the main road, Mosi-oa-Tunya Street, buildings started to appear. Five minutes later, we were dropped off at a small square that seemed the focal point of the town. It consisted of a supermarket, a bank, a few shops, and some bars and restaurants. One sign said: *Zambezi Nkuku: The Number One chicken.*

Small boys had climbed a nearby tree and were shaking its branches. As the green fruit dropped onto the road, others collected them up in baskets. Across the road was one of the town's main attractions, the large and imposing Saint Theresa's Cathedral, a white building with a huge green roof. It proudly boasted that its services were all in English. In front of it were four young men. They were sitting under a red umbrella with the word *Airtel* splashed across it. Two of them favoured beanie hats, but all seemed in a fine mood. One of them said something, and they all laughed.

Further along the street was the Mosi-oa-Tunya Building. At nine storeys high, it was the tallest building in town, used as governmental offices. It was a remarkably ugly thing, reminding me of the 1960s-period office blocks common in many UK towns and cities. We walked past it and found a bar. After sitting down, we thought about what to do next.

"I think we've seen most of the town already," said Angela, swatting a fly away from her face.

I nodded. Livingstone did seem a bit thin on sights. There was a museum across the road, but neither of us fancied that yet. "I reckon," I said, "we finish our drinks and head back to the hotel. Let's lounge by the pool for the afternoon."

"Good plan."

In the taxi, just minutes away from our hotel, the driver braked sharply, and then reversed. The wheels crunched as the gravel spun beneath them. We wondered what was going on, and our senses jumped to high alert.

"Elephant," said the driver, negotiating the dirt track backwards. Just then, a huge male elephant with massive tusks appeared from the edge of the forest. We could hardly contain our excitement despite the danger we were in.

After retreating to a safe distance, our driver paused, watching the elephant for movement. His hand hovered by the gear stick, and his eyes twitched back and forth. The great beast seemed not to have noticed us though, instead contenting itself by munching on some branches at the edge of the track. We had hoped to see big game in Zambia, but had not expected to see it just outside the hotel. A few seconds later, it disappeared into the forest, causing a cascade of crashing sounds.

4

Livingstone, of course, is famous for its high-octane adventure activities, such as bungee jumping, white-water rafting and river boarding. Backpackers from all over the world arrive in the town with the sole purpose of enjoying them all. But there are other activities available for people who do not enjoy dicing with death. One of them is a flight over the falls.

Angela and I ummed and arred about paying $140 each for fifteen minutes, but since neither of us had been in a helicopter before, we decided to go for it. We paid the money and nipped over to a small airfield close to the hotel.

For our flight, two South African ladies, one of whom was obese, joined us. When the pilot beckoned us to his chopper, Mrs

Obese waddled off with surprising speed, and bagged the first-class seat next to the pilot. While Angela and I pondered this misfortune, her friend took one of the rear seats next to a window. Both ladies sat snugly content while Angela squeezed into the economy middle seat, with me at the other side.

"What a flaming cheek," I said to Angela over the melee caused by the engine and whirling rotor blades. "Push her out when we get over the falls."

I could tell Angela was fuming too. I gritted my teeth and tried to manoeuvre myself into a more comfortable position, bitter and resentful. It wouldn't have been so bad if the women had possessed cameras. But no, they were just there to enjoy the ride.

The pilot flicked his switches, checked his dials, increased the throttle, and took off. Within seconds, he steered a course for the falls, and began to give us a running commentary. Soon we forgot all about being angry.

5

"They were discovered by Doctor David Livingstone in 1855, when he was 42," said the pilot as he flew us across the river. "He named them after Queen Victoria."

A few seconds later, we circled around the famous arch-shaped bridge, which served as a border point between Zambia and Zimbabwe. "The steel bridge was built in 1904," said the pilot, "and was the brainchild of Cecil Rhodes, even though he died before it was finished. It is where you can do a bungee jump if you are so inclined." We banked to the left and flew over the magnificent falls.

"This time of the year, there is perhaps only twenty-five percent of the flow that you might see during the rainy season," said the pilot, increasing his attitude slightly. All around us were helicopters and microlights, which the pilot was keeping a good look out for. The four of us stared down at the natural wonder.

Despite operating at only a quarter of its normal capacity, Victoria Falls was exactly as I imagined it to be – torrents of white water gushing over cliffs and ridges, sending plumes of mist high into the air. And then, more or less as soon as the flight had begun, we were back at the airfield, hovering over the parking spot to land.

"I loved it!" beamed Angela. "I want to go up again." I nodded because I had thoroughly enjoyed myself too, despite the best efforts of our fellow seat-hogging passengers.

6

With the fun of the helicopter out of the way, we decided to give Livingstone Town a second chance. After all, the Lonely Planet described it as an *'attractive town with a relaxed ambience and a proud historical air.'* Mind you, in the same chapter it also said the town was *'not much to look at.'*

The taxi dropped us off outside the David Livingstone Museum, a rather grand building featuring a statue of the great man outside its entrance. Like most museums, it contained lots of old skulls, spearheads, pots, and mock-ups of old village life. They had nothing to do with David Livingstone, of course, but were quite interesting in their own way. That said, we quickly sped past them to reach the part dedicated to the man himself.

It was chock full of artefacts, old photos, medals and a whole bunch of original letters penned by the man while on his travels. Livingstone of course had been the first European to see the falls, which he described as having *'scenes so lovely [that they] must have been gazed upon by angels.'*

Although Livingstone's ability at discovering new places has never been cast in doubt, his leadership skills have. People described him as being moody and self-righteous; others claimed he was inept and unorganised. During an expedition along the Zambezi River, Livingstone's own accompanying physician wrote, *'I can come to no other conclusion than that Dr. Livingstone is out of his mind.'* Whatever the state of his mind, one thing everyone agreed upon was that his death was a deeply saddening event.

Angela and I looked at the exhibits detailing the explorer's demise. During his final, fateful expedition, Livingstone caught malaria, and then dysentery. Confused and finding it difficult to have coherent thoughts, he succumbed to the ravages of both diseases in 1873, aged sixty.

Understandably, Britain wanted his body returned home, but the tribe that had looked after him in his dying days were reluctant to give it up. Eventually, both parties reached a compromise. Famously, the tribe said, *'You can have his body, but his heart belongs in Africa.'* So now, Livingstone's body resides in Westminster Abbey, and his heart at the edge of the Bangweulu Swamps in Zambia. It's probably what he would have wanted.

7

In a backpacker shop advertising bungee jumps and helicopter rides, Angela and I inquired about a day trip to Zimbabwe. After all, with it being only across the bridge, it seemed silly not to go.

The middle-aged South Africa man nodded. "Yeah, pal. We can organise that. Pick you up at your hotel, drive you across the border, and then…whatever you like. A trip to the falls? A tour of the city? A chopper ride?"

I conferred with Angela. What exactly did we want to do when we got there? After some discussion, I turned back to the man. "All we need is someone to drive us to Zimbabwe. We'll amuse ourselves for a few hours and then need someone to pick us up and drive us back."

"No probs. Easy tour that one. I'll sort it out for you. A van will pick you up at ten in the morning. How does that grab you?"

It grabbed us very well, and in another moment of impulsiveness, we asked him about day trips to Botswana.

"Yeah, we do Botswana too. You can visit Chobe National Park," said the man. "It's one helluva trip, pal. Done it myself many times. I always come back wanting more from that one."

We shook hands and left his tourist emporium excited at what lay ahead. The next day we were going to Zimbabwe and the day after that, Botswana. Our African adventure was entering a new phase.

As we walked to find a taxi, Angela turned to me. "Isn't Zimbabwe a bit dangerous? And what's to see anyway?"

"I don't think it'll be dangerous where we're going. Plus Victoria Falls town has lots of tourist police. As for things to see, well the falls for a start. We can have a good look at them from the Zimbabwe side. But there are also warthogs."

"Warthogs?"

"Yeah. Apparently they're all over the town."

Angela looked excited.

Chapter 12: Chasing Warthogs in Zimbabwe

Interesting fact: Zimbabwe used to be called Rhodesia. But you probably knew that already.

Almost as soon as we arrived in Victoria Falls town, Angela spotted a warthog. It was walking briskly, snout to the ground, spindly tail to the air, looking as if had important business to attend somewhere.

"Hurry up! Let's get after it," she said. Thus began the Great Warthog Chase of Zimbabwe.

Quick as a flash, we raced towards the corner where we'd seen the hairy beast disappear. With outstretched cameras and flapping arms, we must have looked quite a sight to the citizens of town, some of whom stared as we ran around the bend in hot pursuit of the surprisingly fleet-footed wild pig. It had already vanished though, most probably into some undergrowth. And then, as a final insult to the whole escapade, we were squirted with water from an over-eager hose spinning around a nearby field.

The Great Chase had lasted less than ten seconds. And it had ended in failure.

2

Our day trip to Zimbabwe began at 10am. We were driven to the Zambian border, a disorganized area of blue taxis, waiting trucks and scavenging baboons. After the Zambian customs agent stamped us out, we found ourselves in the no man's land between the only two nations beginning with a 'Z'.

Our driver took us across the bridge, and after a quick stop at the Zimbabwe side of things, we were in, new visas stuck in our passports. Victoria Falls town was only a few minutes away. We said good-bye to the driver and then had spotted the warthog.

Following our disastrous pursuit of the creature, we quickly established the town was full of the hairy, tusked animals.

"Look," said Angela, pointing to a pair of hogs snuffling about at the edge of a dusty road. "And over there!"

I swivelled my head and saw a mother warthog inside a large concrete pipe with her hoglets close by, the youngsters looking impossibly cute. A second later they were gone, retreating into the darkness of the pipe, scared when we'd approached.

A man advanced, proffering a cloth that contained some copper bracelets. "I give you good price," he said.

We looked, but told him we weren't interested.

"Okay, maybe you want a stone hippo?"

It looked quite nice, and so we decided to buy it. It was certainly cheap enough. After handing us our pottery hippo, the man showed us some old Zimbabwe dollars. "How about these?"

Zimbabwe had abandoned its dollar in 2009, after massive inflation had left the currency virtually worthless. I'd read stories about people buying single eggs costing millions of dollars – such was the scale of the rampant hyperinflation. By the end of the run, the government was printing $100 trillion banknotes by the lorry load, causing printing machines to break down, and prices to double every day.

People lost all trust in the Zimbabwean dollar. Workers were receiving trillions of dollars a month in wages, which ended up being worth only a couple of US dollars by the time they could get it out of the bank.

Eventually the government saw the futility of maintaining the Zimbabwe dollar, and began using the US dollar (and its neighbours' currencies) instead. This state of play continues to this day.

After negotiating the man down from his initial asking price, I bought a few different notes, the largest of which was a hundred trillion dollars. It came with a staggering fourteen zeros. After pocketing them, we thanked the man, and walked off to see the sights.

3

Our first stop was the rather posh Victoria Falls Hotel, the oldest hotel in town. Its rooms cost around $300 a night. It reeked of colonial exuberance. It had a large white exterior with maroon trimming. As we entered the large and spacious interior, which was full of animal heads and zebra skins, we felt we had stepped back in time.

In 1947, Queen Elizabeth II had stayed at the hotel, back when Zimbabwe was under British rule. Photos of her adorned a stately passageway along one wing of the hotel. We came to the rear of the hotel and found an expansive patio area. A huge Zimbabwean flag was rippling in the light breeze, and, in the distance, we could see the famous bridge. Plumes of white mist rose into the air near it. It was the smoke that thundered from the falls.

The patio area had a few other patrons, all wealthy-looking Westerners. Most were sipping tea or nibbling on cakes. Instead of having a *high tea* ourselves (an institution at the hotel, involving scones and sandwiches), I opted for a local Zambezi Beer, which featured a large picture of the falls on its sticker. Angela went for a Diet Cola, and while we sipped our drinks in the already searing temperatures of the dry season, we spotted another warthog scampering across the well-manicured lawn of the hotel. It vanished into the bush, trotters going ten to the dozen. No one except us batted an eyelid.

4

Victoria Falls National Park, the gateway to the majesty of the falls, was only a short walk away from the centre of town. After paying the hefty $30 entry fee, we were in, stepping onto the well-signposted trail. Within minutes, we could hear the roar of the torrent, and could feel its spray in the air too. A short walk along a dusty track, verged with deep vegetation, led us to a viewing point.

Nearby stood another statue of David Livingstone. He was gazing out from his rocky plinth in the direction of the cataract.

"Amazing," I said, staring out at the waterfall. Victoria Falls left us in no doubt why it was one of the Seven Wonders of the Natural World. And despite being the dry season, the amount of water gushing over some of the cliff faces was immense. Torrents crashed to the bottom with incredible force. When we peered down, a white cauldron of cascading water was sending clouds of white into the air.

"Look at those people," Angela said, pointing to the other side of the fall, over on the Zambian side. "They look like they're right on the edge."

By straining my eyes, I could see six or seven people sitting in the water, looking like they were having a jolly old time. But what I couldn't work out was how the force of the water wasn't sweeping them over the cusp. Angela was correct; they seemed to be right on the lip. Later we found out they were sitting in an area called Livingstone Island, a small pool of protected water, just behind the edge of the falls.

Angela and I spent the next hour following a trail, visiting the various viewing points. Occasionally we would trample through jungle, filled with small lizards and colourful red flowers. We saw plenty of long-necked birds too, mostly flying out over the falls.

"If this is what it's like now," Angela said, staring at the sheet of white water tumbling over the edge, "imagine what it must be like in the wet season."

"We'd get soaked," I said. "We've come at the right time."

5

Back in the centre of town, we decided to have a bit of a stroll. After running the gauntlet of men trying to sell us things, we found ourselves in a small and untidy park. It was next to a railway track. A trio of warthogs were snuffling in the ground near the track, with a troop of baboons running back and forth further in. Two small children wearing brown school uniform ran to us, gesturing that they wanted their photo taken. Angela duly obliged, and they both giggled when they saw their resulting images digitised on her camera.

We crossed the railway track, and then traversed a nearby road. We walked past a large outdoor craft market specialising in woodcarvings, until we came to a small shopping centre called the *Elephant's Walk Shopping Village*. Inside, hawkers were nowhere to be seen, banished by the presence of a tourist policeman guarding the entrance.

It was quite a nice little shopping arcade, but, apart from us, there were only two other tourists in attendance. The lack of visitors seemed a real problem for Victoria Falls town. In the eighties and early nineties, it had been different. The town had ballooned, catering for the massive influx of adventure tourists coming in. Back then, Zimbabwe was the place to be to see the falls, leaving Livingstone to languish as a dirty backwater town. But then Mugabe dug in his heels, and started throwing his toys out of the pram. It caused the economy to plummet, and the tourists to leave. They moved across the border to Livingstone.

6

"You here for bungee?" yelled a man waiting in the middle of the famous bridge.

I couldn't help but laugh. The thought of doing a bungee jump in my twenties was ludicrous, and now twenty years on, the notion was ridiculous. I'd probably have a heart attack before I even jumped. We told him no, but he was not about to give up. "But you two look so much like jumpers! Come on! Live a little!"

In December 2011, one young Australian woman had done exactly that. Lived a little. Jumping headfirst from the bridge, twenty-two year old Erin Langworthy had approached the river at top speed. Instead of being pulled back upwards though, the cord snapped, and she plummeted towards the crocodile-infested River Zambezi.

Above her on the bridge, some friends caught the moment on video. The sound of shock in their voices is plain to hear. With her legs tied together by the remains of the ruptured cord, Erin found herself being swept towards the rapids. Yet, despite fracturing her collarbone, she managed to swim to the Zimbabwe side of the river, and hauled herself out. How she escaped the crocodiles was anyone's guess.

Accidents like Erin's were a 1 in 50,000 chance, yet we still waved the bungee tout away. We carried on with our hike across the bridge.

We had not intended to walk, of course, but since he had dropped us off at Zimbabwean customs, we had not seen our driver. After waiting in the unforgiving African heat for a while, we quickly realised that there was only one real option – set off and walk to Zambia. Hopefully the driver would pass us and stop.

In the end though, we didn't see his car, but we did enjoy the short walk between borders, because it gave us the chance to appreciate the view once more, even if we were being baked to death. The falls had been well worth the trip, and we had both loved the warthogs. We reached the Zambian border and were stamped back in.

Zimbabwe had been fun.

Chapter 13: Dancing with the Hippos from Hell!

Interesting fact: Botswana's Jwaneng diamond mine is the richest in the world.

"We will have to watch those two hippos," explained the guide, closing the throttle of the small boat we were sitting in. "They want to chase us."

We were bobbing up and down in the middle of the Chobe River, and the hippos were blocking our path. We looked at the large specimens, who were eying us with what I presumed was hippo malice. Only their eyes, snouts and comically shaped ears were protruding above the waterline. Suddenly, like silent assassins, they went under, invisible.

Instead of turning back, our driver told us to hang on tightly. "We will speed through," he yelled, as he pushed the pedal to the metal. Before we could shriek at him to cease the madness, we were off.

Three seconds later, instead of being mashed to death by hippos, or dragged to the depths by crocodiles, we were safe and sound, straining our necks to look behind. Sure enough, the hippos *had* been chasing us, because they were in a new location. With twitching ears, they looked for more prey.

2

Our journey began in Zambia, and after picking up two fellow passengers (a young married couple – Olivia from the UK, David from South Africa), we headed west towards Botswana.

The Zambian border formalities were a breeze, and, before we knew what was happening, the four of us were sitting in a small boat. It was one of the ferries that crossed the thin stretch of river towards the Botswana border. Lines of trucks were waiting to catch the much larger Kazungula Ferry, jamming up both sides of the river. They made us wonder why the people in charge didn't just build a bridge. Surely that would be a better way of conducting business? As it stood, only one lorry could cross at a time, making the whole thing a time-consuming exercise. But not for us; we zipped across in minutes.

Compared to Zambia, Botswana looked affluent. The roads were newer, and the buildings looked better too.

Botswana is actually one of the few African success stories. After gaining independence from Britain in 1966, it started out as one of the poorest countries in Africa. Even so, it held fair and democratic elections from day one. But it was the discovery of huge deposits of diamonds, gold and uranium that turned the tables for the new nation. Massive profits started to roll in, which the government invested cleverly. Instead of lining the pocket of the president and his cronies, Botswana ploughed its new cash into the welfare system, constructing schools and hospitals, and building an infrastructure usually associated with countries outside of Africa.

But all is not good news for Botswana. The country has the second highest infection rate for HIV/AIDS in the world, meaning a quarter of its population have the virus. The situation might end up destabilising the country. As more people succumb to the disease, the bigger the drain on a family's resources it creates. Children are forced to stay at home to look after sick relatives, and therefore grow up uneducated. Others become orphans. In families where adults are unable to work due to AIDS, loss of income becomes a serious problem. The government of Botswana is understandably worried.

3

A short drive from the border, we came to a small town that had a church, a bank and a supermarket. We turned abruptly right to follow a side track through some thick forest. It opened out at a safari lodge, built on the banks of the River Chobe. After a quick drink and a toilet break, we were ready for part one of our Botswana day trip – the river.

The four of us boarded a small motorised boat and, within minutes, we spotted our first herd of elephants. Seven of them were wading into the crocodile-infested river, heading towards a tiny island in the middle. Our guide increased the throttle to get us closer.

I honestly didn't think we would be getting this near to the animals, but the elephants were close enough to touch. They paid us no heed, and merrily reached the island where they began pulling huge mouthfuls of grass to stuff into their oversized mouths. Kingfishers hovered overhead, and beautiful white egrets sat among the reeds. It was, quite literally, an amazing sight, and one I'd only previously seen on a TV screen.

"Hippos," said our guide. We left the elephants and began speeding towards a trio of wallowing hippopotami, heads above the water, bulbous eyes staring at us.

I already knew that hippos killed more people than any other form of wildlife in Africa, and was relieved when our guide stopped a safe distance from them.

These hippos seemed so harmless though, and perhaps even cuddly, especially one of them that was resting its giant head on the back of another. But I knew they could flick into aquatic killing machines in a second if they felt threatened, especially if they felt their young were in danger. Their usual method of mayhem was to tip a fisherman's boat up, and then chop the submerged man in half with their massive teeth. As if reading my mind, one of the hippos yawned, stretching its huge jaws to reveal the pink interior and huge tusk-like teeth.

"This is better than I thought it was going to be," Angela said, as we passed a monitor lizard lazing on a tree branch. Overhead, eagles swooped, and on the riverbank, a mother and juvenile warthog trotted along, oblivious to the crocodiles lurking at the edge. "It's just like being in a nature program."

Everywhere we looked were herds of elephants, gangs of hippos, troops of monkeys, multitudes of antelope, and hundreds of water buffalo, not to mention all the birds. And this was the low season for tourists. I asked the guide about this.

"Yes, most tourists come in July and August. But they will be lucky to see maybe two or three elephants. And the reason is simple: this is the dry season, and the animals are forced to come to the river for water."

4

Scaly eyes and bulbous snouts were all over the riverbank: Nile crocodiles, the guide told us, could grow to 18 feet. I asked him how the elephants and hippos could be in the water with so many crocodiles about.

"The crocodiles do not attack something as big as an elephant or hippo, because they know they would not stand a chance. Instead the crocodile waits for the antelope, or maybe the water buffalo, to come to the water's edge, and then they ambush it for dinner."

Just metres away from the boat, a head popped up to the surface, its reptilian eyes staring, and its jaws parting. The teeth looked deadly, and I wondered whether they ever attacked boats.

"No," said the guide. "They will not attack the boat. Like the elephants, it is too big for them. Just do not dangle your hand in the water. You might lose a finger or two."

We motored around the large river plain, following gentle meanders until the guide headed for an island. It consisted of mainly reeds and grasses. It was full of birds. "Welcome to Namibia!" the guide said, smiling.

The four of us looked at where we were, and saw that it looked the same as any other part of the river chain. There was nothing to suggest we had crossed an international border.

"This half of the channel belongs to Namibia, and you are all illegal immigrants! Please take a photo to record your time in a brand-new country!"

5

Back at the riverfront lodge, I had two quests to complete, a tradition I always undertook in a new country.

The first job was to get some local currency. At the front desk, I asked the lady working there whether she could exchange twenty US dollars.

"Of course," she said, and took my dollars. A minute later, she handed me a few hundred Botswana pula in return. I thanked her and carefully pocketed the cash. I now had a memento to take back with me.

The second job was to taste some local beer. To accomplish this, I wandered to the hotel bar and purchased a bottle of *Saint Louis* beer, the brand of choice in Botswana. I returned to the table where Angela and the young couple were sitting.

"Sorry about this," I said to them, passing Angela my camera. She already knew what was coming. "But I just need to get a short video clip of me drinking this."

Both smiled, amused at what was going on. While Angela filmed, I raised the bottle to my lips and took a sip. After my satisfied '*ahhhh!*' expression, the sequence ended with Angela panning down to the bottle's label. Job done.

I was most gratified when David from South Africa, went off to get some pula of his own, closely followed by a bottle of Saint Louis. I grinned knowingly as his wife took a photo of him with it. A man after my own heart.

6

After lunch, where we learned that David and Olivia lived in East London, a coastal town 700km southwest of Durban, and that

Botswana was their first holiday outside of South Africa, we set off on the second segment of our Chobe Day Trip – the land safari.

Once aboard the open-sided truck, we headed the short distance to the entrance of Chobe National Park. It was heralded by a fine set of skulls, ranging from a warthog to a gigantic elephant. And then we were in, surrounded by scrubland and baobab trees, and, of course, wildlife.

Our driver stopped to point out a dead impala, its body ravaged by predators. Only its head and horns were recognisable. "This has probably been attacked by wild dogs."

Elephants crossed in front of us and antelope sat in the shade under bushes as we bumped along. A trio of giraffes made a timely appearance too, tottering about in such a slovenly manner that we all had ample time to take photos. After twenty minutes or so, the staggering amount of animals on offer grew almost ordinary.

The first time we'd spotted an elephant, all four of us had zoomed our lenses in as far as they would go, snapping off photo after photo. But now, with so many elephants less than ten feet from us, and with so many more around the next bend, and the bend after that, we hardly picked up our cameras. Not that we weren't interested, far from it, but there were literally so many animals that it was pointless trying to get snaps of all of them.

"Grab yourselves a drink," shouted the driver as we bumped over the rough terrain. "They're in the cooler."

David and I were delighted to find it full of beer. We each cracked open a can of Castle Lager, toasting the fact we were in the middle of a wildlife show.

"Cheers," I said.

"Yeah, cheers, mate."

And when the tour finished an hour later, the four of us agreed it had been well worth the $170 each we had paid. We headed back to Zambia as the sun began to set over the African plains. Chobe National Park had been amazing.

7

A day later, Angela and I were enjoying a day of leisure in Livingstone again. Mostly, we lounged by the pool, staring out over the smooth waters of the Zambezi River, or occasionally we would see what the local crocodile was doing. A small specimen, about two feet in length, lurked nearby. Its favoured spot was a tiny stream that fed into the main river. The hotel restaurant overlooked it.

"There it is," I said, pointing down to a shallow part of the water. "Just its head is sticking out."

Angela quickly spotted it, and we watched it awhile. "We couldn't have wished for a more tranquil hotel," she said. "All we can hear is the sound of nature. And those monkeys this morning – I loved them!"

Not long after waking, Angela had opened the curtains to see a small monkey sitting on our balcony. It had spiky brown fur, a dark-brown face, and big black eyes. One tiny paw was curled around a balcony support. As Angela opened the door to give it some almond nuts, the cute little thing scarpered. She put the nuts down on the balcony table anyway, hoping it would return.

It did. With five of its brothers and sisters.

The whole troop scoffed the nuts in seconds, and then waited for more. We tossed some nuts out and watched the monkeys descend upon them like vultures. When they had finished, they sat looking at us again. One of them came up to the glass doors.

"We shouldn't be feeding them," I said, as Angela grabbed another handful of almonds.

"I know. But look at them – they're *so* cute!"

As she opened the door, one of the little buggers jumped from a high beam, and then grabbed the top of the door in an attempt to squeeze through. Thankfully, Angela managed to close the door just in time, sending the furry primate packing. And then we heard a knock at the door.

Bloody hell, I thought. "The hotel management has caught wind of our monkey feeding. They've come to put a stop to it. Hide the nuts," I told Angela, as I headed for the door.

Suitably shame-faced I opened the door, to be confronted by two monkeys sitting on the wall opposite. Both were staring at me. I looked to my left and right, but couldn't see anyone. Had the monkeys knocked on the door, I wondered, flabbergasted at the thought? Were they intelligent and brazen enough to knock on a person's door to demand nuts? But my thoughts were broken because Angela was calling me back to the balcony. I closed the door and shook my head.

Mum and Dad monkey had arrived on the scene, scattering the youngsters away from the balcony. Mum looked bedraggled, possessing a hideous pair of dangling nipples. Dad was larger and brutish-looking, but the distinguishing features were his testicles. They were massive and bright blue. Both stared at us, but with most of our almonds gone, we decided enough was enough, and closed the curtains. We headed down to the pool.

8

After a couple of hours of doing nothing in particular, we grew bored, and caught a taxi back into Livingstone Town. The taxi driver remarked that he was glad to see people actually visiting the town and not just driving through. "Most tourists only see Livingstone from the window of their taxi as they head to and from the airport. I am pleased that you are seeing it on foot."

The town was busier than before, with schoolchildren out and about, and taxi drivers waiting near their blue cars.

Our driver dropped us at the northern end of Mosi-oa-Tunya Street, the prettier part of Livingstone, we had to concede. A couple of colonial buildings, one called *The Capital*, the other *Stanley House,* formed most of the parade, with money exchanges, pharmacies and photo studios taking up most of the ground floor.

One store was closed though, which was a shame. Its ominous green shop sign read: *Freshspot Limited*.

Opposite the parade was a line of craft shops. As soon as we stepped in, men trying to sell us the finest wares at the fairest prices in the whole of Zambia accosted us. It was all in good humour though, and in the end, we bought a warthog made from reeds, a fish made from wood, a lizard made from shaped metal, and a bowl made from polished stone.

And our short time in Zambia had come to an end. For both Angela and me, it had been an incredible and sometimes awe-inspiring time. After all, we'd taken a helicopter ride over Victoria Falls, chased warthogs in Zimbabwe, and seen the wild animals of Botswana. Livingstone, for all its faults, had been a great base in which to do all these things. But now it was time to head back home after our mammoth six-country African extravaganza.

The next trip would be even more audacious than the previous two. It would involve some often neglected parts of Africa, namely Uganda and Rwanda, with possibly the Comoros thrown in too. It would require careful planning, and as soon as we got back to the UK, I set to work.

Chapter 14: Going Solo in Uganda

Interesting fact: Kampala is only 45 miles from the Equator.

Kampala was full of ugly birds. They wandered around parks with their long spindly legs and scrawny necks and sometimes even gathered in trees. As well as being hideous-looking, they were also massive. Marabou Storks were the biggest birds I had ever seen in my life.

Several of the foul things were sitting in a tree near my hotel, and a couple more were wandering about below it. They looked rough and needed a damn good wash. Their heads were the worst part: bald and covered in red blotches and scabs. And then there were the dirty beaks with globules of flesh dangling underneath. If ever there was a less glamorous bird to be seen, I would be interested in finding out about it. Suddenly one flapped its gigantic wings; it was like a pterodactyl taking off.

I smiled. I was back in Africa.

2

"Have you got your malaria tablets?" Angela asked the day before my flight. "And your yellow fever certificate? And don't forget your anti-bacterial wipes!"

"Yes, yes, yes!" I replied, packing my money belt. The belt really was an ingenious thing. As well as being made from fabric (and therefore immune to airport security checks), it had a specially designed, inner section accessible only from an inside zip. When wearing it, no one would guess that it contained money. I carefully folded a few $100 dollar bills and slipped them into the hiding place. It would be my emergency cash.

"And ring me as soon as you get to Kampala."

"I will. Don't worry."

Angela had originally planned on going with me to Uganda, but in the end, with a mixture of family issues, and two cats to look after, she had decided against it. And so I landed at Entebbe International Airport on a solo African adventure. A jaunt that would see me visit five different countries.

3

The airport road was paved, but along its verge was the red dust. It was everywhere, giving the land a copper-tinged edge to its lush green interior. Overhead I could see buzzards and marabou storks riding the thermals, and by the side of the highway, cattle, goats, chickens, pigs, and people competed for space.

We passed a small butcher's hut with a few little oinkers scavenging around outside. Further on was a brick building that advertised itself as a primary school. On its side, in huge black letters, someone had painted *Bic*. Next door to the school was a tiny shack that doubled up as a bar. It proudly boasted that it served *Bell Lager, Uganda's Heritage*. My eyes were drawn to a gigantic billboard. It depicted an unhappy-looking man. The accompanying text read, *Beating my wife destroyed my marriage.*

"Traffeec is bad!" said the taxi driver. "Too many slow trucks."

I nodded, staring ahead. But it wasn't only the trucks that were holding things up; it was the pedestrians, motorbikes and mini-vans too. The vans were usually spewing thick black smoke as they carted their packed passengers towards the capital. I wondered what the police thought of the chaos, but it was abundantly clear what they thought. Groups of them were sitting by the side of the road, armed with semi-automatic weapons, looking bored out of their skulls. They didn't even look up when a motorcyclist carrying a huge wooden cupboard passed them by.

The cupboard was balanced on the front of the thin bike, and it was a wonder the driver hadn't been killed. The only way he could see was by peering through a minuscule slit in one of the panels. The huge cupboard was wider than a bus, and yet he rode onwards, causing a hellish backlog behind him.

4

The Sheraton was located in an area of other plush hotels. It was nestled between a fair number of skyscrapers. Some of them looked quite new.

As the taxi entered the hotel car park, armed security staff inspected the vehicle with long mirrors, checking the underside of the car. After passing their scrutiny, I stepped out into the humidity of central Africa. Within seconds, droplets had formed on my forehead, and so I quickly paid the taxi driver, and ran inside the lobby. The chill offered by the air conditioning was great.

"Welcome to Kampala, Mr Smart," said the suited young man behind the desk, shortening the sound of my surname so it sounded like *smat*. "Your room is ready. Please do not hesitate to ask if there is anything you need."

The room was great, with free Wi-Fi and an expansive view outside. I opened the balcony doors, remembering the monkeys of Zambia, but all I could see were marabou storks.

5

I was outside the hotel staring at a colony of storks lurking in a nearby treetop. The hotel bellboy stood by my side.

"They're big, aren't they?" I said to the young man in the proud uniform and hat.

He nodded. "Yes, they are."

I asked him whether they were dangerous, because I was toying with the idea of photographing one close up. But I didn't fancy the idea of one pecking at me with its bacteria-infested beak.

"No, not dangerous," the bellboy answered. "They will fly away if you get too close."

"What do they eat?"

"They eat the rubbish from the city," he'd told me with a toothy grin. "They eat anything — bones, offal, even shit. But do you know it is illegal to kill one of these birds? Anybody who does will go to jail."

"Really?"

"Yes. The city needs them. Without the storks, Kampala would never get clean."

I spotted a particularly ugly specimen on top of a lamppost. It had a long piece of red stuff, possibly innards, dangling from one side of its hideous beak. As we watched, it flipped it in the air and guzzled it down its scrawny neck.

I thanked the bellboy for his help and wandered over to the group of birds near the trees. The bellboy was right about them; as soon as I got too close, they were off, thundering into the sky as if in slow motion.

I went back inside the hotel to get something to eat.

6

If there is one thing Uganda is famous for, it's for its third president, Idi Amin. After seizing power in 1971, the former military commander declared himself *President for Life,* and renamed Government House as his *Command Post.* He quickly established a reputation for brutality and violence, stamping out dissension with his hob-nailed boots, attacking ethnic groups that did not agree with his measures. Religious leaders, journalists, judges, intellectuals, and even the occasional foreign national, all met with untimely ends at the hands of Amin's henchmen. Their bodies often ended up in the Nile.

Famously, in 1972, Amin declared his *economic war*. In it, he decreed that all Asian people living in Uganda had to leave the country. He claimed the motivation for the expulsion came from God.

The vast majority of Uganda's Asian citizens were from the Indian subcontinent, brought over by the British during the construction of the East Africa railways. Afterwards, many stayed, setting up successful businesses that became important to the Ugandan economy. Amin didn't care about that, and gave them ninety days to get out or else face the consequences. 80,000 people fled, and Amin handed the vacant businesses over to his supporters. This proved devastating. The new owners mishandled things badly, and soon large swathes of the manufacturing industry collapsed. Uganda was in trouble.

To prop himself up, Amin secured money from the Libyans, and then converted to Islam. Because of this, the Saudis gave him a pile of cash. When he expelled every Israeli from Uganda, the Soviets became his best friend too, supplying him with weapons and armaments.

Despite this, Idi Amin was becoming a paranoid man, worried that people wanted to usurp his power. Thus began a period of terror in Uganda.

People began disappearing from the streets of Kampala with alarming frequency. A pair of shoes left by the side of the road soon came to symbolise Idi Amin's oppression. Kidnappers made their victims remove them before whisking them away. In total, experts believe that up to half a million people were killed during Amin's regime.

Due to Amin's unpredictable nature, his circle of trusted advisors began to shrink. Some defected, but most were executed. Amin declared war on neighbouring Tanzania, believing they were the source of his troubles.

Libya sent in 3000 troops to bolster the Ugandan army, but then found itself making up most of the front line. Ugandan army units were driving supply trucks in the opposite direction, filled with plunder.

In the end, the Libyans abandoned ship, leaving Amin's troops to fend for themselves. Six months later, Tanzanian troops reached Kampala and Amin fled, initially to Libya, then onto Saudi Arabia. He lived in Jeddah until his death in 2003.

7

The next morning, I wandered around the corner of the hotel until I reached the Independence Monument. It was a structure that was on the back of every Ugandan shilling. The monument featured a tall man wrapped in some sort of bondage. In his arms, he held a child reaching upwards. A sign just in front read, *Idlers not allowed around this monument.*

That was a strange thing to warn people not to do, I thought idly. I glanced at my watch and headed back to the Sheraton. In ten minutes time, I was being picked up for my tour of the city.

The guide turned out to be a young woman called Imelda, who informed me she was also a university student. "Normally I work in the office," she said. "I answer phones and do the paperwork. But today, the boss man has allowed me to lead a tour myself. I hope I do a good job for you."

Our first stop was the mighty Owino Market, a sprawling conglomeration of stalls and shacks, tightly packed with humanity. According to Imelda, there were half a million stall holders in the shopping hub.

"It is the main market of Kampala," she told me, as she tottered about in her heels, openly attracting the attention of quite a few men. "And it is always busy like this."

I wandered up to one stall that sold jeans. They looked second-hand, and I was right because some of them still had Oxfam charity tags attached.

Imelda joined me. "This market gets lot of old clothes from rich countries. You probably thought that England's old clothes would be given away free, but that is not how it works in Africa. Almost all charity clothes will end up in markets like Owino. This is bad for our local textile industries. They cannot compete with these low prices. Many go out of business, sending their workers out onto the streets without a job, or any means to feed their family."

8

As we shuffled our way deeper into Owino Market, we passed a stall selling huge rat traps. They looked powerful enough to break a man's arm.

Next we came to a fruit and vegetable section, perhaps the busiest area of the market. Mangoes, jackfruit and papayas were laid out on wooden tables, with brightly clothed women hovering over them. All looked at me as I passed. I continued following Imelda through the rabbit warren until we came to another large clothing area. Here, men sat sweating over ancient sewing machines.

"Mista!" a male voice shouted. "Come here, cheap T-shirts!"

I looked and saw a man pointing at his stall. Like the jeans, the T-shirts were all second-hand. I thanked him but turned back to Imelda.

"Many people's livelihoods are tied to this market," she explained. "And without it, they have no source of income." She paused, bending down to inspect a piece of ginger. A second later, after deeming it unsatisfactory, she put it down again. "But there has been talk of pulling the market down."

"Why?"

"Mainly because of a powerful bus company that has influence over the government. They say they need the area to park their buses. They do not care that the people who use this market will have nowhere to sell their goods."

On the way to the Kibuli Mosque, we passed motorbike after motorbike parked by the side of the road, their owners either chatting or lounged asleep on top of them. They were the ubiquitous boda-boda drivers, taxis on two wheels. I asked Imelda how much a boda-boda driver might make in an average day.

Imelda shrugged. "Maybe ten thousand shillings."

That was about £2.50. Not a lot for day's work in the fume-filled streets of downtown Kampala, where fatalities involving boda-bodas made up the vast majority of traffic accidents.

9

The Kibuli Mosque was large and white, and had a dark green dome in the middle. On its front in bold lettering was: *None to be worshipped but Allah.* The mosque sat at the top of one of Kampala's many hills, and was a haven of peace against the honking traffic down below.

Imelda and I climbed out of the car, and while I took some photos, a teenage girl appeared. She had a stooped back, and walked with a peculiar gait. At first she started to head towards me, but when she spotted Imelda, she veered away. Five minutes later, I was done taking photos, and turned to see Imelda chatting to the girl. Both were holding hands and smiling.

"Do you know each other?" I asked.

Imelda nodded. "We are friends, but I've never met her before. We make the friendship while we wait for you. She lives close by, and I'm going to give her a gift."

Back at the car, Imelda fished about in her purse, and handed the girl a few shillings. After saying thank you, she shuffled off, watching us depart.

"The next mosque we will visit," said Imelda, "is called the National Mosque, but most people know it as the Gadhafi Mosque. Idi Amin started it in 1972, but it was not finished until 2006, when Libya finally paid for it. It will take maybe twenty minutes to reach, depending on the traffic."

To pass the time, I looked outside. More red dust. I had never seen so much red dust in all my life. It even coated some of the fruit by the side of the road, giving the mangos and bananas a rusty hue. One shack was clear of the dust though. It was stacked with metal dishes, kettles and colanders. A frail woman sat near them, staring at her feet, absently brushing sand away from everything.

10

The Gadhafi Mosque was large and light brown. It had a huge minaret and a fetching archway at its entrance. If the arch had been painted in bright colours, it would've looked like a rainbow. Imelda's choice of clothing was to let her down, though. Her bare legs did not go down too well with the people in charge of the mosque, and she had no choice but to relinquish control of me to an official guide.

Mohamed, my perpetually smiling guide, led me inside the vast, but empty, interior. It was capable of holding five thousand people, he told me.

Mohamed looked to be in his early thirties, and was clearly proud of the mosque. Sweeping arches led my eye upwards towards the beautifully patterned dome.

"The chandeliers were made in Egypt, and the windows were brought from Morocco," he said. "And I am responsible for singing the call to prayer five times a day! Come, I show you Holy Koran!"

Mohamed led me to a massive, glass-fronted cabinet containing the most revered document in Islam. We both stared at the fancy Arabic writing, none of which I could understand.

"If you like, I could sing this page for you?" Mohamed said, a hopeful expression on his face.

I nodded and gestured for him to start.

He had a good voice, that much was clear, and when he had finished, I gave him a short round of applause that made him smile.

"You think my singing is good?"

"Yes," I said. "You have a beautiful voice. You should be on TV."

Mohamed laughed. "On TV? You think? I am greatly honoured to hear this."

Twenty minutes later, I was back with Imelda, driving away from the mighty Mosque.

11

"Tell me please," Imelda said. "What do you think of Kampala?"

At that particular moment, we were passing rickety stalls peddling car parts or piles of bananas. I saw a sign saying *Curious Undertakers*. Everything was passing in a whirl of colour.

I thought it was great. To me, Kampala was what I'd expected it to be: chaotic and *African*. People trying to eke out a living with whatever they could get their hands upon, and it excited me being there, among the madness, albeit from the safety of a passing car. I said all this to Imelda.

"Yes, I think I understand what you mean," she said. "Sometimes I wish I could see Kampala from new eyes."

We arrived at a grand-looking building that turned out to be the Buganda Parliament Building. It was large and stately, with an impressive array of windows, and finished with a big spiky turret on the top. A marabou stork was perched on the roof.

A young man called Lutalo was acting as our guide around the parliament building. He was about Imelda's age, and all of us were standing at the entrance to the building, next to a grand statue of a man wearing some sort of elaborate headwear.

"This is Mutebi II," explained Lutalo. "He is the current king."

I stared at the hat again. It looked like an elongated fez, with a large feather poking out of the top. I turned to Lutalo. "I had no idea Uganda even had a king."

"Yes. The monarchy was put into exile in 1966. But in 1993, they were reinstalled. Of course, the power they once enjoyed is gone, but they still have the authority to legislate on non-political issues. Come: I show you inside."

The entrance hall had a set of square engravings on a wall. Most of them featured animals, but a few were of plants, and other objects that I couldn't make out. They were totems, Lutalo explained, and each one represented a different clan of Uganda.

"There are fifty-two clans altogether, and I am from the Reed Clan." He turned to Imelda and asked what her surname was. After she'd told him, he smiled. "Ah, the Elephant Clan! Very big clan."

Imelda nodded and smiled.

Lutalo gestured at the totems. "But there is something interesting to remember about the clans," said Lutalo to me. "No one from the same clan may marry each other."

Lutalo pointed at a totem, and asked me what I thought it was. I stared at it awhile, and thought it perhaps looked like a few coiled snakes, or maybe a set of seashells. Lutalo laughed. "No, you are wrong. It is shit, defecation."

Beside me, Imelda made a sound of shock and began to giggle. Clearly the Shit Clan was news to her as well.

We moved into a room that reminded me of a tiny version of London's House of Commons. In fact, it turned out to be the governmental room, and featured a set of benches on both sides. "When the king is here," said Lutalo, "he will sit on that special throne at the end of this room."

I asked him whether he'd ever met the king.

"Many times," Lutalo said grinning. "But I have only shaken his hand once. Afterwards, I did not wash my arm for two weeks! During that time, many people wanted to touch my hand so that they could touch the king too."

12

The twin towers of the Saint Mary's Cathedral looked disappointing after the glitz of the mosques and parliament building. Its best feature was the view it offered, and the small, dusty stall selling cold drinks near its entrance.

I ignored the cathedral, and went over to some nearby railings with my drink. Marabou storks circled everywhere, riding the thermals over the red dusty streets and traffic jams of downtown Kampala. Even from high upon in the hills, the trumpeting of vehicles still managed to make its way to my ears. The heat was intense too, a never-ending blast of humid air that seemed to cling to my skin like a warm towel. In the distance, on another hill, was a plume of smoke. I watched it gently rise into the air in an almost vertical line. A breeze would have been welcome at that precise moment.

"Come," said Imelda. "It is time to go back to your hotel."

13

After informing Imelda that she had been a great guide, she drove off, leaving me to find somewhere for lunch. Along the way, I picked up a local newspaper, the *Red Pepper*. It claimed it was the newspaper of the year. When my meal of boiled fish and rice arrived, I began reading with interest.

The main news story involved a plot against the current Prime Minister, but the headline that caught my attention read: *Man Burns Bonkmate's House*.

Bonkmate? Was that a real word? And if it was, did it mean what I thought? I began to read with glee.

At 10.45pm, the previous evening, neighbours noticed a strange man banging on the door of a woman called Eunice. These unnamed observers hypothesised that the man was one of Eunice's many bonkmates. As the gentleman knocked away, he also demanded to be let in. When no one answered, he grew angry and then, as the neighbours watched, he set fire to Eunice's thatched roof. The paper juicily wrote: *Eunice, who was known for thigh vending in the area, had already sneaked to another sugar daddy.*

Thanks to the café's free Wi-Fi, I typed bonkmate into Google, and quickly discovered it was a distinctly Ugandan term. And it did mean what I thought. And, also thanks to Google, I read that a twenty-year-old male student from Kampala was searching for a bonkmate to enjoy a one-night stand with. He described his appearance as 'not too short' but later caught himself out by stating his height was actually 4'11". He finished his message by making it clear he was not fussy: *I don't care the way you look, just make sure you are not too fat.*

The Red Pepper also contained some interesting advertisements. *Manhood Enlargements,* I learned, could be completed in three days. Or, if that didn't sound like much fun, then an artificial penis could be delivered to your home in only one day. A lady called Senga Akugoba could solve the perennial problem of *Lost Lovers* in the quite-precise 42 hours – guaranteed, and could also arrange for *Dry Women* to get their fluids back in a mere thirty minutes.

For the perplexing procedure known as *Elongating of the Twin Towers,* Senga promised it would take no longer than four days, and if anyone wanted their *Men Weapons* to be armed and primed, she could do it in less than a week. As well as this bewildering array of services, she also offered *Customer Attraction, Get for you jobs* and the intriguingly sounding *Pre-Mature Ejaculation.*

I noted down her number and closed the newspaper.

14

My short time in Kampala was nearly at an end. And despite the grime, the ugly birds, the snarling traffic jams and layers of smog, I had loved my short time in the Ugandan capital. Kampala might not be the Pearl of Africa, as it sometimes calls itself, but it was certainly a nicely polished bit of rock. I returned to the hotel to pack for part two of the trip: Rwanda.

Chapter 15: Remembering the Past in Rwanda

Interesting fact: Rwanda is also known as the Land of a Thousand Hills.

Mugisha and Yvonne were brother and sister. In 1994, they were aged three and five. The photo showed them smiling without a care in the world. Both had been hacked to death inside their grandmother's home because they were from the wrong tribe.

Another child was smashed against a wall. He was two at the time of his murder. And when the death squads arrived at four-year-old Umutoni's home, they stabbed the little girl in the eyes and head.

The Genocide Memorial Museum was unbelievably depressing, especially the final room full of children's ghosts and photos. But what got me the most was that it had only happened in 1994.

2

The difference between Kampala and Kigali could not have been any starker. It was clean and well-manicured, the red dust was at a minimum, and there was not a single marabou stork anywhere. The airport road was in top condition, and the cars driving along it looked new and expensive. Also, unlike the Ugandan capital, there were no roadside shacks filled with masses of humanity. Here the people looked affluent, and seemed to be going somewhere, rather than just hanging around. So far, Rwanda was impressing me.

Getting to Rwanda involved a dash of time travelling. My Rwandair flight had departed from Kampala at 11am but arrived in Kigali at 10.45, fifteen minutes before I'd taken off. This neat trick was due to a combination of Rwanda being one hour behind Uganda, and a flight lasting only forty-five minutes. But, as great as all that was, passport control was even better. I didn't need a visa to enter the country. Just a stamp, a smile, and I was in.

The Top Tower Hotel looked like the abode of a criminal mastermind. It had gold panelling on the outside, and a distinctive dome on the top. The evil, Bond-villain look was finished with a powerful radio antenna sticking up from the middle of the dome. Goldfinger would have found the building much to his liking. I checked in and unpacked my things.

3

Half an hour later, I was in a taxi to the centre of the city, thinking of the two grenade attacks that had occurred only a few days previously. One was at a city centre market, the other in the outskirts of Kigali, and though no one had been killed, the UK Foreign Office was advising British citizens to be extra vigilant, especially with the commencement of the official genocide remembrance activities.

The taxi dropped me off outside the Hotel Des Mille Collines. During the genocide, this particular hotel had been where 1268 people had taken refuge to avoid the slaughter outside. The manager at the time, Paul Rusesabagina, managed to accomplish this feat by bribing the death squads with money and alcohol, putting his own life in perpetual danger by doing so. His actions were later immortalised in the 2004 movie *Hotel Rwanda*.

The Hotel Des Milles Collines was posh. I wandered through its entrance into the pool area at the rear. During the genocide, people had used the pool's contents as drinking water.

The patio was full of people, mainly white tourists enjoying lunch. It looked so serene. Attentive waiters were hovering around the guests, and over by the pool, a couple of young women lay sunbathing. A beautiful little orange and green bird landed on a nearby flower, its plumage shimmering in the sun. I sat down and ordered a drink. How different it all was.

Half an hour later I was wandering around the centre of Kigali, trying to follow my pathetic Lonely Planet map. It might as well have been a blank piece of paper for all the use it was. Half the buildings on the map were no longer there. In the end, I shoved it in my pocket and began to walk aimlessly.

"You want map?" said a voice to my left. He'd evidently seen me struggling with the one I had.

"Actually," I answered, "yes I do."

Unfortunately, the man only possessed large ones of the entire African continent. Not much help to me. I shook my head and walked away.

4

Kigali looked pleasingly modern. It had some nice shiny skyscrapers, and lots of shops. Men walked past me wearing white shirts and dark ties, sometimes carrying briefcases, whereas women were splashed in colourful attire, much the same as ladies across the whole of Africa. There was no rubbish on the streets (plastic bags were banned in Rwanda), but, in contrast, some of the trucks chugging along the roads were sending out thick trails of black smoke. Things were changing in Africa, I mused, but the trucks would always be the same.

I passed a large glass-panelled building called Centenary House, and was accosted by a man trying to sell me a newspaper; he had a bundle of different ones draped over his arm. I brushed him off, but then a small boy rushed towards me.

"Hey mista!" he implored. "Please give me franc! I hungry! 100 franc buy me bananas. Please mista, please!" He followed me along the street, while I tried my best to ignore him. I knew if I gave him anything, then other beggars would immediately surround me. He eventually gave up and ran back to the wall he'd been sitting on.

Other Western tourists were facing the same thing, but none of them were giving money either. I was actually surprised at the number of tourists in Kigali. Compared to Kampala, the city was a tourist Mecca.

I continued walking downhill towards a large roundabout with a fountain in the middle. It was called Place de L'Unite National, a busy area of green surrounded by roads leading off in all directions. Another child rushed up to me, this one a girl of perhaps four. She didn't speak any English, and tried to take my hand. Eventually she gave up when I crossed a road.

In the centre of the roundabout, I found a bench and sat down. Over on my right was a huge shiny skyscraper that dominated the city's skyline with its modern blue glass exterior. The Kigali City Tower was an entertainment centre full of shops, bars, restaurants, and even a multiplex cinema. It looked like something you would see in Dubai. After a sip of water and a wipe of my brow, I stood up and headed towards it.

Like most African cities I'd been to, people were everywhere. Most were shopping, but others were trying to sell lottery tickets, or flog leather belts to passersby. In Kampala, hardly anyone had stared at me, not even little kids, and that was in a city where I seemed to be the only white face. Here, Westerners were everywhere, and yet the stares came thick and fast. Whenever I paused to take a photo, people would glare at me. I moved onwards, past the Kigali City Tower, up a slight hill, until I realised I was lost. The high-walled buildings around me meant I could not establish my bearings.

"Bloody Lonely Planet," I hissed to myself, causing a few people to look. And where were all the street signs? Surely a capital city should have some street signs?

The heat was getting to me, and now that my mood had darkened, I began to notice the red sand. The volume of it was nowhere near Kampala's, but there was still enough to get between my toes and rub me the wrong way. Every now and again, I would hear a beep as a motorbike-taxi driver tried to attract my attention. I waved them all off and traipsed further up another hill.

Twenty minutes later, I found myself back at the Hotel de Mille Collines. I had no idea how I'd found it again, but at least I now knew the way back to my own hotel. I set off walking, ignoring the beeps and the occasional blast of black smoke. After forty minutes of humid hiking, I arrived back at the Top Tower.

5

I was the only person in the hotel restaurant. For a moment, I wondered whether it was closed, but then I noticed a waiter at the far end watching TV. I coughed, and he jumped in surprise. After turning off the television, the man rushed over to me.

"I'm so sorry, sir, I did not know you were there."

I told him not to worry, which seemed to calm him.

"You want to eat, sir?" he asked. It sounded almost like a plea.

I nodded, causing him to smile. He turned around to face the sea of empty tables and said, "Please follow me."

The table he picked was by an open-window, overlooking the street. There was a nice breeze flowing in, so I was happy with his choice. While the waiter went off to get a menu, I sat down and stared outside, once again noticing the black-and-white checkerboard edging to the road. It reminded me of a grand prix racing track. A chugging truck passed by, closely followed by a motorbike.

The menu came, and while I perused it, the waiter returned to his corner. I looked up and saw him smiling. So were the other four waiters.

During my meal of beef strips and rice, all five continued to gaze at me. The looks were not threatening in any way, but slightly off putting. To break the ice, I called one of the waiters over, and the original man came charging.

"Yes, sir?"

"Can I have a beer please? Do you have any local ones?"

The waiter nodded enthusiastically. "Yes we do! We have Primus or Mutzig! Both are tasty Rwandan lager."

I opted for a Primus, hoping the waiters would get bored of staring, but if anything, my order of a local beer had brought about a rush of excitement. When I took a swig, all waited expectantly. I felt like a goldfish in a glass bowl.

Trying to ignore my audience, I ate my meal in silence, promising myself to find somewhere else to eat the next day. Briefly glancing up, I saw a sixth person had entered the show, the chef. Finishing my last mouthful of beef, I gave him a thumbs up. A waiter patted him on the back, and he looked graciously proud. I paid the bill and returned to my room.

6

The next day I was in a taxi to the Genocide Museum. Along the way, I got chatting to the driver, a friendly man who spoke good English.

"If you like," he said, as we drove along, "when you have finished at the museum, I can take you to Congo? It take three hours, and cost $200. I take you there, and bring you back."

The Congo! Now that would be an interesting side trip. And even though $200 seemed a bit steep, it might be the only opportunity I'd ever get to visit the Democratic Republic of the Congo. Besides, I could probably barter him down a bit.

"I will not be able to take you across the border," the driver admitted. "I do not have the papers to do this. But we can drive to Gisenyi Border, and you will be able to get another taxi to take you to Goma. It is the town on the other side. I will help you with this."

I did a quick mental calculation. If I was done with the Genocide Museum by about 10.30, I could be at the Congolese Border by half past one. A couple of hours to wander around, and I'd be back in Kigali by about 7pm. Very doable. I told the driver I'd think about his proposal after I'd visited the museum.

7

"Starting on 7th April 1994, and lasting for one hundred days," said Diane, the young museum guide, "Hutu militia groups known as Interahamwe murdered up to a million Rwandan Tutsis."

Historically, the Tutsis had been the minority ethnic group in Rwanda, yet had controlled most of the country's power. That was until 1962, when a Hutu-led government was established, forcing Tutsis to flee to neighbouring Uganda and Congo. There they formed a rebel army, which made frequent attacks into Rwanda. This civil war lasted for many years, but hardly anyone in the West noticed. After all, it was just another tin pot African nation fighting over some tribal ancestry or something.

Things continued like this until 1993, when an uneasy peace agreement was put in place. To help broker this, a contingent of UN peacekeepers was flown to Kigali.

Behind the scenes of this peace treaty, a massacre of unprecedented scale was being planned. Even as ministers discussed the ins and outs of the agreement, half a million machetes were secretly being brought into Rwanda.

Diane explained more: "Newspapers, and then the radio, sent messages to Hutu people that it was okay to hate Tutsis. This hate propaganda grew so commonplace that it became normal, part of people's daily life. And because many people in Rwanda were illiterate at the time, these radio broadcasts became important to them. Educated people were telling them to hate Tutsis, to fight with them, because if they didn't, their lives would be made unbearable. They believed what they were hearing."

The General in charge of the UN peacekeepers, a Canadian man called Romeo Dallaire, soon realised that things were not going to plan, especially when a plane landed at Kigali Airport full of weapons and ammunition bound for Hutu militia. He warned his superiors that there was a possibility of an attack on the Tutsi population of Rwanda. His superiors ordered him to leave the shipment of arms alone. Dallaire had no option but to sit back and wait.

8

On 6th April 1994, a plane carrying the Rwandan and Burundian presidents (both Hutus) was shot down on approach to Kigali Airport. Everyone died in the crash. This proved to be the spark to ignite the genocide.

A contingent of fifteen UN troops was sent to protect the Rwandan Prime Minister, a woman by the name of Agatha Uwilingiyimana, who was next in line to take control of the country. When the UN peacekeepers arrived, they found Hutu troops already surrounding where she was hiding. As the prime minister and her husband tried to escape, Hutu troops murdered them both.

The UN troops came under attack too. After surrounding them, the Hutu commanding officer ordered the peacekeepers to surrender or else be killed. Completely outnumbered, the UN troops (ten Belgian and five Ghanaians) agreed to the demands. They were quickly taken prisoner.

The Rwandans released the Ghanaians, but drove the Belgian men to a military base. After accused them of shooting down the president's plane, the UN troops were left to the mercy of irate Hutu militia men.

Four of the Belgians were hacked to death straight away; the rest managed to escape to a vacant building, grabbing a weapon in the process. In their hastily-constructed barricade, the UN soldiers held out for three hours, until a grenade ended their resistance. All ten bodies were stripped and then mutilated. Genitals were removed and stuffed into mouths. Some bodies were dismembered. The Rwandans left their remains outside to be discovered.

Belgium responded immediately. It pulled all of its troops out of Rwanda. The crippled UN forces were now left with only 270 men. It was time for the genocide to begin.

9

Diane led me to the exhibits, where I saw the first of many harrowing photos. Corpses were everywhere, and a lot of them were children. One horrendously depressing photo showed a room full of bodies. One of them was clearly a motionless little girl, her arm wrapped around her dead mother.

"Please watch this short video," said Diane, pressing a button on a small monitor. "You will see some of the children who survived the genocide. They are now adults."

The first person interviewed looked like any of the young women I'd seen in Kigali the previous day. But she had a sadness in her eyes that was upsetting to see.

'I watched as my mother was killed,' the young woman said on the screen. 'They told her to lie down, and then they shot her in the head.'

The scene shifted, and a young man appeared. He had the same sad look of the previous speaker.

'My mother and sister were killed, and I watched it happen. The militia stabbed my mother with a spear, and, afterwards, they chased my sister as she tried to escape. The Interahamwe caught her, and then threw her into a deep latrine. They threw rocks at her until she stopped screaming. They made me watch.'

Diane switched the screen off. "This happened every day for one hundred days, and it was only the lucky ones who were killed quickly. That was the easy way out. Sometimes people paid the Interahamwe to shoot them, so they could get it over with. You see, Hutus liked to inflict torture and torment on Tutsis. Often they hacked at a person's thighs and left them in agony for a few hours. Then they might come back and hack off an arm, before leaving them once more." I looked at a photo of a dead man half inside the window of a car. He'd probably been trying to flee the death squads. Wounds were visible across his back.

"There were so many bodies in Kigali," Diane said, "that dogs began to eat them."

I wondered why the Tutsi population simply hadn't escaped Rwanda when they'd had the chance. After all, there were plenty of warning signals.

"Many did," explained Diane. "But roadblocks were quickly set up all over the city. No one could get past them, unless they could prove they were Hutu. These roadblocks became prime killing grounds, and so Tutsis didn't go near them. Instead they tried to hide. That's why the Interahamwe began searching houses."

April 9th saw one of the worst mass killings. With death squads hacking and clubbing people to death all over the city, a hundred Tutsis, including many children, fled into a nearby church. It didn't offer any sanctuary, because the Interahamwe simply followed them in and started hacking.

By chance, a couple of Polish UN Peacekeepers saw what was going on. They contacted their base commander for assistance, but were told that no help would be forthcoming. Similar reports were coming in all over Kigali, and, besides, the UN mandate was non-intervention. When the killers departed the church, they left a scene of unimaginable horror behind. Sliced limbs, severed heads, twisted corpses, and a lake of blood.

On the same day, a thousand European troops arrived in Kigali. It was only the third day of the genocide. But instead of helping the people of Rwanda, the troops merely supervised the withdrawal of European personnel. As these Westerners retreated from their compounds, many saw their Tutsi co-workers murdered before their eyes. And, everywhere in Rwanda, the killing, the raping, the torturing and the total lack of humanity continued. But still the world looked on, and did nothing. The genocide continued for the next three months, with four hundred people dying every single hour, which equated to almost ten thousand a day.

On 17th July 1994, Tutsi forces finally took back control of Kigali. This resulted in thousands of Hutus fleeing into Zaire (now the Democratic Republic of the Congo). One hundred days in hell had finally ended, but the country was left crippled, and the capital overrun with corpses. Only now did the UN decide to send some in the reinforcements, but, as General Dallaire, the UN commander in Rwanda, bluntly stated, it was too much, too late. The damage was done.

Bill Clinton on a visit to Kigali in 1998 acknowledged that the world had let Rwanda down.

10

Back outside, I found my taxi driver waiting for me. To be honest, I was no longer in the mood to travel to the Congo, and I told him this.

"Perhaps next time," he said gracefully. He dropped me back off in the centre of Kigali.

This time I couldn't help but see the city differently. I began to study the people around, wondering if they had known anyone who had been killed.

While waiting to cross a busy road, I noticed a man on the other side staring at me. He looked to be in his early-thirties, which meant during the genocide, he had been a teenager. I looked away, making a show of glancing at my watch. His haunted expression was disconcerting. When I looked back, he was still staring.

What did you see during the genocide? I wondered sadly. *And what part did you play in it? Were you one of the lucky ones who managed to hide from the Interahamwe, or were you perhaps part of them?* A sudden break in the traffic broke the spell for both of us. We crossed each other heading in opposite directions.

11

After lunch in a cafe just off Place de L'Unite Nationale, I decided to flag down a motorbike taxi, to take me back to the hotel. The thought of travelling on the back of an African motorbike worried me, but the thought of walking back worried me more. Placing the helmet on my head, I climbed behind the driver and put my feet on the supports. We were soon off, tearing through the streets of Kigali at top speed.

After a while, I became used to my balanced position and actually started to enjoy the wind rippling over me. Perhaps riding on the back of a motorbike was the way forward, I thought. I arrived at the Top Tower fifteen minutes later, safe and sound. It was almost time for part three of my East African adventure: Mombasa, Kenya.

Chapter 16: Motorbikes and Prostitutes

Interesting fact: In terms of GDP per capita, Kenya is just below Bangladesh, but just above Nepal.

The smell of ripe human sweat hit me like a bomb. But these were not the backstreets of downtown Mombasa, or a crowded minibus hurtling towards the frenzy of the ferry terminal; no, this was on the plane from Kigali.

The culprit was a large, middle-aged white man from South Africa. Even the short walk to the aircraft brought him out in a rich lather of dripping perspiration. Once aboard, he hefted his luggage into one of the overhead bins, and unleashed a torrent of odour so foul that I thought I might collapse. And then he flopped down beside me, large patches of sweat visible all over his T-shirt. It was going to be a long flight.

2

Our approach into Mombasa was heralded by lightning flashes, which lit up the night sky like a scene from a disaster film. Half an hour later, I was in a minibus on the way to the centre, approaching a roadblock that looked like it belonged in a different movie: this one depicting an armed coup.

Lengths of steel wire were suspended between oil drums, the darkness briefly illuminated by an open fire. Just enough flickering light revealed a man hidden in the shadows armed with a rifle. My driver slowed down as he approached the makeshift barricade, but the man with the rifle simply opened the wire up, and allowed us through.

The streets of downtown Mombasa seemed largely deserted as we sped through them. Nearly every shop was closed, many with armed guards posted outside. A few lonesome men wandered the streets, cigarettes offering points of light. Wondering what Kenya would have in store for me, I sat back and stared straight ahead.

3

Mombasa is Kenya's second-largest city, and its most important port. Because of its location on the Indian Ocean, it has always been an important trading centre. Spices, precious metals and ivory have all passed through the city at one time or another, traded from as far away as India and China.

By the 19th century, Mombasa was in the hands of the British, as part of the British East Africa Protectorate. Slaves toiled away in plantations, and ivory caravans became a common sight. But nowadays, the city attracts wealthy tourists. Its tropical, palm-swept beaches burst with luxury hotels, full of Westerners enjoying a slice of paradise before being whisked off to their high-end safaris.

My hotel wasn't on the beach; it was right in the centre. The Castle Royal Hotel was a large whitewashed structure with a sprawling veranda that doubled up as a restaurant and bar. I had breakfast in it and then waited.

"Hello, are you Mista Jass-on Smatt?" said a man in his late twenties. He was wearing a T-shirt patterned with elephants and lions. Around his neck he wore an official tour guide badge.

"Yes," I answered, shaking his hand.

"Then this is very good! I am Amos, your tour guide for this morning. If you are ready, we can begin."

4

Bathed in daytime sunshine, Mombasa didn't seem as threatening as before. In fact, it seemed to be a healthy mixture of African and Asian, with a sprinkling of spice from Arabia. Even the Castle Royal Hotel had managed to incorporate some Arabian-influenced arches into its colonial façade.

"The first thing I will show you are the giant elephant tusks," said Amos, leading me along a busy street called Moi Avenue. All the shops were open and people filled the areas in front of them. A man on the other side of the road was pushing a large cart filled with plastic water bottles. Auto Rickshaws and cars sped past. It reminded me a little of Delhi, only without the ingrained grime.

The tusks were impressive. Four of them criss-crossed the entire road, forming a huge, curving letter 'M' (for Mombasa, presumably).

"They are not real, of course," said Amos, "They are made from aluminium, and covered in white paint. They were constructed in 1952 when Queen Elizabeth came to visit."

Our next stop was a Hindu Temple. It was a creamy pastel colour, emblazoned with splashes of green, pink and blue. It reminded me of an ornately decorated wedding cake. Inside was torture.

The three large murals on the wall depicted scenes of pure torment. For instance, drinking alcohol would bring about an endless agony in hell, one picture warned. Horned devils were pouring boiling water down the offender's throat, and, behind them, demons armed with skewers were stabbing people. Crocodiles and sea serpents munched on their remains. If a person ate a juicy steak, then they could look forward to snaggle-toothed demons putting them inside a large pot of boiling water.

"I'm glad I am not a Hindu," said Amos.

5

Our next stop was the exotic-sounding Spice Market. Unfortunately, it turned out to be a common-or-garden fruit and vegetable hall.

"It used to be an Omani slave market," explained Amos as we wandered through. A few fruit hawkers tried to attract my attention by pointing at their mangos or passion fruit, but we continued walking past them. "And it is where male slaves were once brought. Next door was for the female slaves. It is now a meat market. Come, I show you."

Strips of red meat, and other things that may have been testicles, dangled from stalls inside the rank-smelling meat hall. Men with large machetes were chopping into carcases and then discarding the bones by their feet. In one dark alcove sat some huge white bones with bits of flesh hanging from them. Each one was streaked in red.

"Camel," said Amos when he noticed me staring. "This market sells mainly goat and camel meat."

We wandered into the old town of Mombasa, which was mainly Arabic in nature. It resembled Zanzibar's Stone Town. Muslim ladies wandered the alleyways, and children played with marbles in quiet corners. In upstairs windows, washing hung from small lines, and all around were tight jumbles of telephone wires crisscrossing each other. And then we came to the ocean.

It looked gorgeous, a deep azure only possible to see in the tropics. A couple of boats were bobbing about near the edge, and a teenage boy, armed with a fishing line, sat perched on a rock. Across the other side of the inlet were a line of pastel-coloured buildings, most of them with arched windows and flat roofs. A bulbous minaret stood above the line of dwellings. This was the Mombasa I had imagined. I took a photo for posterity.

6

Fort Jesus is Mombasa's biggest tourist attraction. Dating from the 16th century, the Portuguese had built it as part of their expansion plans into East Africa. They constructed it from coral, and then filled the walls with cannons and turrets.

The colour had long since faded. Instead of being a pleasing brownish-pink colour, Fort Jesus was now a black-streaked brown. But what remained of the fort was still impressive, with much of the original walls and battlements still intact.

Amos and I stepped into the grounds. The open-plan ruins clearly showed where barracks, slave rooms, and prison cells had once been. Stone steps led to the battlements, and thin archways offered views of the ocean.

Suddenly, a platoon of purple-attired school children arrived. They seemed more interested in me than in any of the ruins. One bold boy, aged about ten, came up and asked if I was from America. Behind him, about eight of his friends gathered, all grinning.

"No, England," I replied.

His look of confusion meant that Amos had to explain what I'd said.

"Ah," the boy said. "Wayne Rooney! Manchester United!" He returned to his friends laughing and pointing at me. The boys then headed towards a cannon.

"The fort was under constant attack," explained Amos, as we stared out across the Indian Ocean. "And was fought over, on nine separate occasions. When the Omanis eventually won it from the Portuguese, they made it taller by a few metres."

"Why?"

"The Omanis were much taller."

Twenty minutes later, we headed to the exit. Amos turned to me. "So that concludes the city tour. But if you like, we can continue this afternoon. I will show the *real* Mombasa, on the other side of the river, and not just the tourist places you have seen so far. It is not part of the official tour...but you will enjoy it, I'm sure. What do you think?"

Hmm, I thought. Not part of the official tour? And why was that? And did I really want to entrust myself into Amos's hands when I hardly knew the man? He could take me somewhere and rob me. On the other hand, I had no plans for the afternoon, apart from wandering around by myself, and Amos seemed a trustworthy type, so I was torn.

Amos sweetened the deal. "I will arrange for us to go on the ferry, and I will also show you the beaches that Mombasa is famous for. But it is up to you."

It sounded like a plan, so I arranged to meet up with him after lunch.

7

While Amos returned to his tour company office, I wandered into the hotel bar. There were a few other customers already sitting around, but I managed to find an empty table and took a seat. Ten minutes later, a young woman entered and sat by the bar. She was wearing a short, tight grey dress, and was by herself. Ignoring her, I began to read a newspaper I'd bought earlier.

The main story was about how useless the government was. It claimed that, for every person doing a meaningful job in Mombasa, there were nine others doing nothing. As an example, it said that the government employed five electrical engineers who, between them, had forty-five tea boys, messengers, and other assorted lackeys. *Why are we paying these people?* the newspaper asked. Why indeed.

"Hello, please can I sit with you?" said a voice. It was the girl I'd seen at the bar. I'd been so absorbed in the story that I'd not noticed her approach. I was momentarily flummoxed, and didn't know what to say. I glanced at the other people in the bar, but no one was paying us any heed. I shrugged and nodded, wondering what else I could do.

She was aged about twenty, I reckoned, and pretty. She sat down and crossed her legs, making a show doing so. Next she smoothed her tight top, making sure it showed just enough cleavage to make the message clear. She looked up and said, "Where are you from?"

I told her I was from England, even though I didn't want to engage her in conversation. My food was about to arrive and the last thing I needed was a prostitute by my side.

"England, eh? I am from Dar es Salaam." She re-crossed her legs and leaned forward to shake my hand. "I am staying at a hotel not far from here."

Over at the bar, I saw the barman glance over, and smile knowingly. Instead of saying anything more I decided to act dumb and read my newspaper. Hopefully she would get the message and leave.

She didn't.

My meal came, and still she stayed put. Out of courtesy, I offered her a chip but she declined, saying they were bad for her figure. And for the next fifteen minutes, I ate my meal and pretended to read, even though the whole thing was a major ordeal. When I was done, I asked for, and then paid, the bill. Then I stood up.

"We go now?" the girl asked hopefully.

I shook my head and rushed off. I even forgot my newspaper.

8

I met Amos and explained what had happened during lunch. He was wearing his own clothes now, I noticed; his tour company ID card was nowhere to be seen.

Amos shook his head. "This girl would have seen your wedding ring, but not cared. Come, we catch tuk-tuk to ferry terminal." Amos flagged one down (Chinese-made I noticed), and then we were on our way.

The terminal turned out to be a flurry of activity, with stalls and hawkers trying to flog things to passing foot passengers. Cars and trucks were queuing up in the haze, and Amos and I jostled and squeezed with the crowds, waiting for the signal to board. Soon the announcement came, and we entered the fray. A man just ahead of us was carrying a couple of chickens, and, in front of him, another man was carrying a pile of cardboard on his head.

Like the ferry crossing in The Gambia, Amos and I hit the top deck for the journey. But unlike the Gambian crossing, this one only took five minutes.

A similar parade of shacks and stalls greeted us at the other side, but Amos and I ignored them, and headed for a line of waiting motorbike taxis. After some negotiation, Amos told me to get on the back of one. Two days previously, in Kigali, the thought of jumping on the back of a motorbike had worried me — and that had been on decent roads with a crash helmet. Yet here in this part of Mombasa — where the roads were little more than dirt tracks — I jumped on the back without even thinking about crash helmets.

What the hell, I thought. It was time to live a little. A few seconds later, we set off down a bumpy orange back street, passing simple dwellings with tin roofs. Amos was a passenger on the bike in front, and as we drove along, getting deeper into the township, I began to have a nagging feeling. Had I made a mistake in agreeing to this tour?

Suddenly we turned left, and then right, and then right again. Or was it left? I couldn't remember. A woman by the side of the track was hand washing some clothes. We quickly passed two men sat in a doorway doing nothing in particular. Suddenly an old man spotted me and stared as I sped past.

Where was Amos taking me? I had assumed it would be some sort of African village, not this. What if I was being driven somewhere nasty? What if this was some sort of elaborate kidnapping scheme? After all, Amos was working freelance, without his company or anyone else knowing where we were. I was literally flying solo on the back of a motorbike through a place where no other Westerners dared to tread. We turned up another little back street, and I grimly hung on, wishing I'd stayed back at the hotel.

Suddenly Amos's motorcycle veered sharply right, and, a second later, so did we. The track was even bumpier now, flanked by more tin-roofed shacks. A woman carrying a baby on her back gazed at me as I passed, and I wondered whether the safe house was around here somewhere. They could keep me hidden for months until the ransom was paid. Or perhaps they were the middle men for Somali militia. Somalia was the next country up from Kenya, and, as a Brit, I would be prize booty for them.

We came out of the residential area and onto a main road with the ocean on my left. I was glad we'd left the township behind. Half a mile down the road we finally came to a stop and Amos climbed off his bike.

He came towards me. "Come," he said, "I show you the beach."

Perhaps I wasn't going to be kidnapped by Islamic militants after all. I followed Amos towards a quite beautiful beach, and calmed down. A few monkeys and a troop of small school children hovered under a large tree. It was hardly prime kidnapping ground.

I gazed out at the tranquil Indian Ocean. It looked like it belonged in a holiday brochure. I realised how foolish I'd been. Amos was a married man, for God's sake, and he had a two-year-old son. Also, he wasn't a Muslim, he was a Christian, he'd already told me.

"Tell me," Amos asked. "What did you think of the journey through the village?"

I paused, thinking of what to say. I couldn't exactly tell him I thought I was being abducted, so instead told him I'd enjoyed it, which I suppose I had. After all, this was what travel was supposed to be like – breaking the boundaries of everyday life, sampling something new, stepping out of comfort zones.

"I'm glad you liked it. Not many tourists get to see what you have seen. Come, let's get a beer to cool ourselves down."

"Good idea."

We climbed back onto our motorbikes.

9

Twenty minutes later, the motorbikes dropped us off at a bar near the ferry terminal. It was called the King Fisher. Instead of sitting in its stuffy interior, we decided to sit outside. We both took healthy gulps of Tusker Lager, savouring the cooling liquid after the hot and dusty journey on the motorbikes. After another sip, I asked Amos if he'd ever been to Europe.

"No. But I would like to visit one day. However, I would not want to live in Europe. It is too expensive, and it has lost touch with its traditions. The country I would most like to live is the Congo. Outside of Kinshasa, it is largely untouched, and still holds the deepest African customs."

Amos took another sip of his lager and looked wistful. "My dream would be to move my family there, build our home on the banks of the River Congo. I would clear the land down to the brown river so that we could grow whatever food we needed, and be able to catch fish. But I cannot see this ever happening. Congo is becoming dangerous, and anyway, my wife likes living in Mombasa."

After finishing our drinks, Amos and I crossed back over the river where I was to experience a brand-new form of transport. It was the mini-bus taxi. Lines of them stood waiting for departing ferry passengers. Before I had chance to say anything, I was bundled aboard one, pressed shoulder to shoulder with the humanity of Africa. And then with a hard hand slap on the side of the vehicle, we were off, forcing our way through the jam of other vehicles. Amos was sitting behind me, staring out of the window. For him, this was totally normal.

The journey was a madcap adventure of beeping, and sudden, jolting stops. I stared outside at the scenes of Mombasa passing by my window, marvelling at Africa. Fruit stands, corrugated metal, colourful ladies, and scorching sun. The minibus stopped, and a push of people boarded, squeezing aboard the already packed-out vehicle. Money was passed to the driver's assistant as we set off. I smiled and turned to Amos. He nodded and gave me the thumbs up. Five minutes later, we climbed out and stood on the pavement. The mini-bus taxi juddered off into the traffic of downtown Mombasa.

"Thank you, Amos," I said. "I really enjoyed this afternoon, and am glad you were the one to show me." I handed him a hefty tip.

"Thank you," he said as we shook hands. "And if you are ever in Kenya again, please seek me out. I would love to show you many other things in Mombasa. Today we have only scratched the surface."

As I entered the Castle Royal Hotel, I kept a wary eye out for the hooker from earlier. Thankfully, I couldn't see her anywhere, and escaped to my room to pack. Mombasa was hot, sweaty, sometimes annoying, often eye-opening, but, above all else, fun. The next part of my adventure would be just as interesting though, I hoped. My 5.30 am flight would take me to one of the poorest countries in the world, the Comoros.

Chapter 17: Where is the Comoros?

Interesting fact: Almost half the population of the Comoros is under 15.

In the Comoros, I reached the lowest ebb of my trip around East Africa. Perhaps it was to do with the lack of sleep or maybe the fact I'd had enough of the heat and humidity of Africa. Or perhaps I simply missed home. The rain didn't help much either. Thick, dark clouds had covered the entire country on our approach, and as the Kenya Airways jet descended below them, the beaches looked black and angry, pounded mercilessly by ferocious waves.

2

Thirty minutes before landing on Grand Comoros, it had been a different story. My flight had taken a scheduled stopover in Mayotte, the French dependency that had once been part of the Comoros. The ocean surrounding it was a mesmerizing palette of tropical blues. But then we'd taken off and flown into the rain clouds.

"Why you here?" asked the security official inside Prince Said Ibrahim International, the main airport of the Comoros. I looked at the man, sweat dribbling down my forehead due to the lack of air conditioning inside the poky terminal building. People gathered around to listen.

It was a good question.

The Comoros was one of the poorest nations on Earth, despite its enviable location in the Indian Ocean. And it wasn't exactly politically stable either. Since independence from France in 1975, the Comoros had endured a stupefying twenty-four coups, earning itself the nickname *Cloud Coup Coup Land.*

The tiny African nation intrigued me, though. Everyone knew about Mauritius or the Seychelles, but most people didn't know about their little cousin: the Comoros. Nobody I knew had ever been there. And that was like a magnet for me. Off-the-beaten-track places were my favourite holiday destinations. But my mood was not good. I was dog-tired and wanted to go to sleep.

"I am a tourist," I replied to the official.

He raised an eyebrow. "You come to Comoros as tourist?"

"Yes."

The man studied my colourful Comorian visa, issued in a side room only moments before. The people around me strained their necks to look too. Finally the man nodded, and returned my passport. "Enjoy stay."

3

Outside the terminal, I faced the usual taxi madness. A car pulled up, organised by a taxi manager on the verge of bursting a blood vessel every time a passenger appeared. As soon as I got in, he banged on the window, telling the driver to move away quickly.

The airport road was a thin, pot-holed slither of black tarmac flanked by dense green jungle, offering only brief glimpses of the ocean. The traffic was light, which was a blessing considering the large cracks at the edge, and the goats munching on the undergrowth. The windscreen wipers were working overtime to keep the rain at bay, but in the distance, Mount Karthala loomed, its top half hidden under an opaque layer of cloud. Mount Karthala was one of the largest active volcanoes in the world. It had last erupted in 2006. I peered nervously at it, wondering whether magma was brewing deep within its bowels.

"Premiere fois en Comoros?" said the taxi driver in French. He was asking if it was my first time in his country.

"Oui," I affirmed. We passed dwellings made of corrugated metal and dirty grey breezeblocks. Women walked along the roadside edge, with wrapped bundles on their heads, adding splashes of colour: a purple sarong with a zigzag pattern here, a bright orange veil there, all were in direct contrast to their men folk, who favoured simple T-shirts and white skull caps.

Nearing Moroni, the tiny capital of the Comoros, the houses added paintwork and sometimes small porches. Men gathered under corrugated verandas to enjoy conversations while women hurried past them. The sand beneath their feet was black and dirty-looking, though highly fertile. It was everywhere, a gift from the volcano.

As we hit the outskirts of Moroni, my driver pointed out the main sights as we passed them: the rundown Comoros TV station building, the walled Presidential Palace, and an electrical substation. "Votre hotel," he said, turning off into a side road. I strained my neck to see. It didn't look good.

4

There was no fridge, no air-conditioning, but it did have a dirty brown towel hung in the dank bathroom, and a toilet that had no flush. Instead it utilised a bottle of brown water. The worst thing though was the lack of a safety deposit box.

I placed my suitcase next to the prison-issue bed, and sat down, holding my head in my hands. It was no good; I couldn't go to sleep knowing my belongings were not safe. If my passport was stolen, what would I do then?

I pulled at the cupboard doors again, which remained stubbornly closed despite my best efforts. The only saving grace I could think of was the safe might be inside it. I decided to go down to reception to find out. As long as there was somewhere to store my valuables, then I could put up with the hot and sticky room for the two nights I was in the Comoros.

The hotel's reception was a TV room with two lounging men staring vacantly at the screen. When I explained to the woman behind the small desk about the locked wardrobe, she summoned a slack-jawed man who looked like a character from a *Scooby Doo* cartoon.

Inside my room, the caretaker immediately went to the wardrobe and tried to pull it open by brute force. When this didn't work, he had a bit of a poke around with a key he'd found in his pocket, but when that didn't work either, he stepped back and regarded the cupboard with consternation.

After rubbing his chin, he finally nodded and smiled at me, revealing a toothless and inane grin. After digging around in his pockets again, he produced a small metal rod that he placed in the gap between the cupboard doors. I watched incredulously as the galoot simply forced the lock. It gave way, and the door swung open to reveal its empty contents, similar to the man's skull I felt.

When a mosquito buzzed past my ear, I decided enough was enough. I was not staying in a place where Handyman Joe could pilfer my belongings. I packed my things and left. Half an hour later, I was safely ensconced inside the best hotel in the Comoros, the Itsandra Beach Hotel. Hell had turned into Heaven.

The contrast was astounding. The Itsandra was where visiting diplomats often stayed. As night fell and the rain stopped, I sat in the outdoor bar watching fruit bats overhead, and listening to the ocean battering the shoreline below. Even the obligatory power failure could not dampen my new-found sense of adventure.

5

Since independence, the Comoros has endured at least twenty-four coups.

The first coup occurred in 1975, less than a month after independence. An armed group, led by a French mercenary called Bob Denard, removed President Abdallah, and replaced him with Prince Jaffar. Six months later, the Comoros had its second coup. The prince was ousted, and replaced by one of his deputies, a mysterious man known as Mr Solih.

Mr Solih had no experience at leading a nation, and one of the first things he did was to appoint a fifteen-year-old boy to be his chief-of-police. When a soothsayer told him that a white man with a black dog was going to kill him, he ordered the mass shooting of every black dog on the island. Despite these signs of instability, Solih managed to cling onto power for two years, enduring seven coup attempts in the process. But then Bob Denard returned to the Comoros with 43 men.

The French mercenary successfully removed Mr Solih (who was killed in the coup) and replaced him with a President Abdallah (the same man he'd helped oust in the first coup.) Denard paraded Solih's body through the streets of Moroni with a black Alsatian by his side. The soothsayer's prophecy had come true.

President Abdallah ruled for the next eleven years, a miraculous amount of time considering, but this was due to a shrewd move he had made upon accepting his presidency – he made Bob Denard the chief of his Presidential Guard. During these years of relative stability, Denard converted to Islam and became a citizen of the Comoros.

In a by now well-overdue coup, Abdallah was overthrown and killed in 1989. His assassination coincided with his decision to disarm the Presidential Guard. Naturally, Bob Denard was blamed for the death, and, in the ensuing battle, he was injured. French paratroopers had to evacuate him to South Africa.

Mr Solih (president number 2) had a brother, who now decided to step into the limelight. With Denard out of the way, for the time being at least, the second Mr Solih staged his very own coup, and became the new president. Surprisingly he lasted until 1995, until Bob Denard decided to holiday in the Comoros again. Instead of arriving with sun cream and a good book, the Frenchman came with guns and coup-staging equipment.

This time the French government stepped in, finally putting a stop to the madness. They took Denard back to France, telling him that his coup-taking days were over. A Paris-backed man became the new president and lasted until 1998. When he died, it was time for another coup.

Surprisingly, it didn't involve Denard. It was down to the colonel in charge of the army this time. After taking control of the nation, he promised democratic elections. They were not very democratic though, because he rigged the election and won. But then something odd happened. Five years later, the colonel willingly stepped down to make way for another man. The new president's nickname was the Ayatollah, because he had once studied in Iran. This was a momentous occasion for the Comoros, because it was the first time that power had been transferred peacefully.

With the Ayatollah holed up in the Presidential Palace, another coup occurred, this time on the neighbouring island of Anjouan. A different colonel tried to seize power. Troops were sent in, and the imposter fled to Mayotte by speedboat.

In 2010, the Ayatollah stepped down peacefully, and was replaced by his deputy. And since then there has been no more coups. And as for Bob Denard, he died in 2007, aged 78.

6

The next morning I got a phone call asking me to go down to reception. When I got there, the pleasant lady behind the desk informed me that the credit card payment I'd made the previous evening had failed.

"Do you have another card we can try?" she asked.

I wondered why my card had failed. In Mombasa, it had worked just fine, and I knew there was plenty of credit available on it. I looked at the lady and shook my head. "No, sorry, I don't."

"I see. Then maybe you can pay by cash?"

"I don't have enough." I felt the first stirrings of alarm.

"Well there is a machine over there. Perhaps you will try it?"

According to the invoice the woman passed me, I owed the hotel 150,000 Comorian francs (£250). In my wallet, I had about 50,000 francs that I'd managed to change at the airport on the way in. Upstairs in the safe I had a hundred-dollar bill, a twenty euro note, and some assorted Kenyan and Ugandan shillings, all of which was still not enough. Besides, I needed some money for my tour of the city later that morning, as well as for the taxi back to the airport. If push came to shove, I decided, I could probably cobble together enough cash for the night I'd already stayed, but then would have to find somewhere else for the night. That thought made me shudder. Even the hotel without the safe was out of my price range now. The thought of staying somewhere worse was beyond comprehension.

I walked over to the machine with a terrible feeling of dread, but at the same time marvelling that the Itsandra Beach Hotel had its own ATM. As far as I could tell, it was the only one on the island. I popped my card in the slot, hoping for acceptance, but it ejected it with a message telling me the transaction could not be completed.

I felt sick.

I wondered if I should beg for mercy, and tell the woman I would pay as soon as I returned to England. I could even offer to pay double! To stall for time, I pushed the card in for another go. But like before, it spat it back out. And it was at that moment that I remembered my money belt. A wave of euphoria washed over me. I was saved!

Not caring that the woman was watching me, I removed my belt and unzipped the secret compartment. And there they were, four crisp, hundred-dollar bills! I could've kissed each one in turn.

I walked back to the desk and placed them on the desk. The woman smiled and picked the slightly warm notes up. After working out the exchange rate, she told me I now only owed 3000 francs. I got them out of my wallet and settled up. I was staying at the Itsandra.

7

Half an hour later, I met Omar, an affable guide in his mid-forties. Unlike many of his countrymen, he wasn't wearing a *kofia* – a round, brimless hat. Instead he preferred a smart cotton shirt with a pen poking from the top pocket.

"We don't get many British tourists," he told me as we walked to the car. "In fact we don't get many tourists at all. But those who do come are usually French."

Our first stop was a tiny settlement just south of Moroni called Iconi, which had once been the old capital of the island. It consisted of a few dwellings, a large white mosque, and some old ruins dating from 16th century Omani rule. Goats ran free around the ruins, as they did over the whole island, but my attention was drawn to the lava-encrusted beach. A naked man was wading into the ocean to bathe. Towering above him was a tall black cliff face. Hundreds of years previously, women had flung themselves to their deaths to escape slavery at the hands of Malagasy pirates.

I asked Omar whether the Comoros had ever suffered at the hands of modern-day Somali pirates.

"Yes," he answered. "Not long ago, pirates captured one of our fishing boats. The pirates realised the boat was low on fuel and headed for Madagascar. As they neared the coast, the pirates hid below deck, instructing the Comorian crew to say they were lost and needed fuel. But they did not realise that the ship had already been reported missing by the authorities. Soldiers were sent aboard and captured the Somalis."

A kilometre south of Iconi, Omar led me to the edge of a small lake. "This is where witchcraft sometimes happens," said Omar ominously. "People kill chickens and throw them in. Then they collect the water; they say it can cure illness."

As we drove away from the lake, I noticed another young woman with a grey painted face. Ladies such as her were a common sight in the Comoros. She was walking along the side of the road with an older woman, presumably her mother. She looked like a corpse.

"The beauty mask," Omar told me, "is to keep their skin young and soft. It is made by mixing sandalwood and coral in water."

8

We parked in downtown Moroni, a hive of bustling market stalls set under large bright parasols. The capital's architecture was a mixture of Islamic and Swahili, endless arches with the occasional minaret. Flecks of litter by the edge of the road spoiled the look somewhat, as did the faded and cracked paintwork, but the ladies of Moroni countered this. Seated among piles of bananas, papayas, mangoes and jackfruit, in their colourful cloth wraps, their shrill laughter drew the eye. Whenever anyone noticed me, they stared and sometimes pointed. No one seemed hostile though, merely inquisitive why a white man was visiting their market. A stranger from far away.

Omar led me down some steps and into the heart of the medina. It dated from Arabic times. It was a shaded place full of mothers watching over playful children. Grey stone walls curved around the myriad of passageways, with white paving stones leading the way. The shade came from corrugated metal overhangs, and the colour came from the doorways, often painted in vivid blues and reds.

"The Comoros is a matriarchal society," said Omar as we strolled through a winding alley. "The women own the houses and land. After she dies, it is passed to the eldest daughter, and so on. That is why the birth of a first daughter is a momentous occasion for a family."

I asked what would happen if a family had no daughters.

Omar nodded. "In that case, the family will normally adopt a girl, perhaps from a sister or cousin."

We came out of the medina into an open area by the sea. A large rusted red ship lay in the shallows, and a group of boys played in a small boat near it. Behind us was the most photographed building in Moroni, the Friday Mosque, dating back to the early 15th century. It was large and white, with an arched arcade running across the first two floors. I could see why people liked it.

"There is a new, bigger mosque now," Omar said. "But this will always be my favorite."

9

We drove northwards. After a few kilometres, we stopped and began a climb through a jungle trail that led to the Ruins of Itsandra. Goats ran ahead of us, and large snails and shimmering bronze lizards littered the ground. Fingers of bananas hung from nearby trees.

"An Omani sultan owned the palace," explained Omar as we trudged our way uphill. "But there is not much left – a few guard towers, a sleeping chamber and a royal meeting hall."

Undergrowth covered most of the ruins, with leaves and branches poking through gaps in the walls or feeding their way into what had once been doors. But the views from the ruins were stunning: a sea of vegetation spreading to the aquamarine of the Indian Ocean.

"Come," said Omar. "We go see the fishermen now."

On the road, a cavalcade of three shiny vehicles passed us, beeping loudly. The middle car had its windows blacked out, and for a fleeting moment I thought it might be the President of the Comoros fleeing the latest coup. But it turned out to be the Sudanese ambassador trying to ramrod his way to the airport.

The fishermen were only a few minutes away, out in the surf, clumped together in a tight jumble of wooden boats. About forty of them, I estimated. Omar and I walked onto the beach to see them closer.

"The fish resemble sardines," said Omar as we walked across the yellow sand. "When cooked with coconut milk and breadfruit, they are delicious."

A group of women stood with trays of fish balanced on their heads, about to go to market according to Omar. Out in the ocean, the fishermen toiled with hand lines, like they had done for hundreds of years. Young boys congregated at the edge of the water, while women sat on upturned boats waiting for more fish to come in. All around, exotic conversation carried over the sound of the waves.

10

For the remainder of my final evening in the Comoros, I watched brooding storm clouds gather, which soon turned into torrential thunderstorms that shook the walls of the hotel. As I packed my bags for my flight to Dar es Salaam the next morning, I thought again of the question the security official had asked me.

Why you here?

Well now I could answer him properly. It was simple really: the Comoros offered a slice of traditional Indian Ocean life. It offered the intrepid traveller the chance to see an old town that could rival the ones in Zanzibar and Mombasa. It offered tranquillity, natural beauty, and it offered the real threat of volcanic eruption. But even more than that, the Comoros offered exclusivity. How many people could say they had visited the Comoros? Well, I could.

I cringed at my outburst when I'd first arrived on the island. I'd been a spoilt tourist having a tantrum about a dirty towel when most of the island lived in poverty. But at least I'd changed my initial impression of the Comoros, and seen the island for what it was worth.

One more stop, I thought. One more stop and then I would be leaving Africa.

Chapter 18: The Final Stop – Dar es Salaam

Interesting fact: In Bradford, UK, there is a sunbed establishment called Tans-in-here.

Dar es Salaam International Airport had the most convoluted visa-on-arrival system I had ever encountered. First of all, I had to fill in a couple of lengthy forms that asked me to repeat the same information twice. As I did this, a young man waited by my side, peering over my shoulder.

The man looked lost and confused, but he was making me feel uncomfortable by his close presence, so I asked him what he wanted. The man simply nodded.

Ignoring him, I filled in my forms. Maybe he was waiting to use my pen. After I'd finished my forms, the man passed me his passport and *his* forms. He had an imploring look on his face. Ten minutes later, I'd filled in everything for him, and passed them back. He accepted them gratefully, just as a woman tapped me on the shoulder. She too proffered her passport and forms, but I shook my head and walked away. I'd be there all day otherwise.

Then the real confusion began. Crowds of passengers were waiting at customs control. A piece of paper was pasted onto a glass window. It displayed the various prices for the different types of visas available: two-day, three-day, thirty-day, multi-exit, US citizens, Canadian, Irish, and a whole plethora of other combinations were possible to buy. After trying to decipher it, I wandered to a nearby hatch, but the lady inside shook her head and gestured that I should move away.

I shook my head in anger and frustration. What was I supposed to do?

2

"This must be your first time in Dar?" said a man's voice. It belonged to a tall South African. I nodded, and he smiled knowingly. "What you need to do, is pass your things to *that* guy over there."

I looked at where the man was pointing. A security guard was stood by himself, seemingly with nothing to do.

"That guy deals with everything, but no one will tell you that. You'll be here for hours unless you give him your things."

I did as instructed, wondering how I'd have worked it out without the South African's help. The guard took my passport and forms, and they quickly disappeared around the other side of the hatches. I began to wait like everyone else.

"Thanks," I said the South African.

He nodded. "I've been here forty minutes already. It's an insane system, if you can even call it a system."

Periodically, a passport would appear; that lucky owner allowed to proceed. Occasionally an official would summon a person to a hatch to answer questions. Afterwards, they would return to the holding point, wondering whether the answers they had given had been deemed appropriate. The South African man was right; there was no system. It was luck of the draw. And where my passport was, I had no idea. Suddenly the South African man was called over to a hatch. A minute later, he was clutching his passport like a trophy.

"Good luck," he said to me as he headed towards border control. I watched enviously as he escaped through it. The young man I'd helped earlier had also got through. It didn't seem fair. I stood and seethed.

A group of Chinese tourists arrived and looked bewildered. And who could blame them? They stood looking this way and that, until I took pity on them, and explained what I knew. They gleefully smiled at me, one of them shaking my hand vigorously.

Twenty minutes later, a new pile of passports appeared from somewhere, and the crowd thinned. I shuffled my feet, huffing and puffing.

"Jah-son...Smat?" said a woman's voice. I turned around and saw an official in uniform summoning me towards her booth. Somehow my passport made it across to the customs desks. With a stamp and a big African smile I was through, almost an hour and a half after landing at the damned airport.

3

Compared to the Comoros, Dar es Salaam, Tanzania's largest city, was back to civilisation. The roads were in good condition, and large billboards advertising the latest Samsung phones and computer tablets spoke of modernity. But being a large city in Africa meant the traffic was hellish. Cars, trucks, motorbikes and small ice-cream vans were causing black-fumed tailbacks at every set of traffic lights. Taking advantage of this though were the hawkers trying to sell maps, mops, newspapers and cashew nuts. I lost count of the number of times there was a tap on my window.

With only a few hours of daylight left in Dar es Salaam, I wasted no time in venturing out into the streets. It was hot and humid, but I didn't care. I was leaving the next morning, and it would be the only chance I'd get to see the city. Armed with my Lonely Planet map, I headed away from the hotel. I was soon lost.

4

Getting lost in some cities is no big deal. Just look for a street sign, or perhaps a passing policeman, and you're soon on your way. In Dar es Salaam it was not so simple. Street signs were non-existent, and the only police officers I could see were busy directing traffic. Besides, lingering too long in one place would draw street hawkers. But worse than any of that was the heat.

Whenever I stopped to look at the map, the breeze generated by my walking pace would cease. Immediately, I'd break out into a terrible sweat. The only way to keep cool was to walk. So I kept moving until I arrived at a church. According to my map, I should have been at a supermarket.

The church was good, though, and looked like it belonged in Europe somewhere, perhaps Germany, especially with its tall spiky spire covered in red tiles. The only thing spoiling the illusion were the tropical palm trees sprouting up in its grounds. I noticed a sign reading: Azania Front Lutheran Church. I looked at my map and saw where I was. And then it made sense: my map reading skills were so abysmal that I had set off down the wrong street immediately after leaving the hotel.

5

With the Indian Ocean to my right, I finally had a real bearing to work with, and so I wandered over to a wire fence so I could see the water. The port area was full of container ships making it look dirty and almost unwelcome. The other side was nicer, though, with a set of wooden boats moored under some distant palm trees.

"You want taxi?" asked a man jumping up from underneath a shady tree. Sweat was dripping down my back and my shirt had unsightly wet patches, but I waved the man away. I crossed a road and passed through a small park favoured by napping men. I stopped to look at my map again. I was actually hoping to find something called the Askari Monument, a bronze statue built in honour of African troops killed in World War I.

Five minutes later, I passed a small statue of what looked like a soldier. It was in the middle of a roundabout, but seemed too small and insignificant to be the Askari Monument, and so I ignored it until I came to a street full of market stalls. People sat underneath brightly coloured parasols, with piles of bananas, mangos and cigarettes for sale. Other people offered shoe shining services, and some women had weighing scales in front of them. I bypassed them all, trying to keep the breeze flowing.

"Taxi?" said another man.

"No thanks!" I said jovially, even though I probably looked like a man about to die from sweat poisoning. "I'm fine!"

He nodded and sat back down under a tree.

I passed a tall, thin clock in the middle of another roundabout, and stopped to study the map. There was something called the Clock Tower marked on it, but this thing couldn't be it because it was hardly a clock tower, it was more of an advertising box with a clock on the top. It was advertising *Panasonic Batteries*. I plodded onwards, this time passing residential blocks and furniture shops. After fifteen minutes of trudging, I had to concede I was utterly lost.

6

The heat was intense and I was cursing myself. After another half a mile, I gave up and wandered towards a bunch of waiting taxi drivers. Three of them jumped up immediately, vying for my custom, but I gestured to the first man who had made eye contact with me. Euphorically, he led me to his vehicle.

"Okay," I said before we jumped in. The man's eyes flickered from my sodden T-shirt to my face. He was possibly assessing whether I had malaria or something. "I want you to take me to the Clock Tower, the Askari Monument, the ocean, and then a supermarket so I can buy some Kilimanjaro Lager. Then to my hotel, the Holiday Inn. Okay? That's five stops."

The man nodded. "Whatever you say, boss. But it will be fifteen thousand shillings." He was staring intently at a line of sweat dribbling down my face. I must have looked a total wreck. He was probably going to drive me straight to a hospital.

I nodded, fifteen thousand shillings was about six pounds, which seemed okay for such a journey, especially through the congested streets of downtown Dar es Salaam. I jumped in the back, wound down the window and was soon basking in the relief from the breeze as we moved off.

The Askari monument was just down the road and had in fact been the same statue I'd seen earlier. Mentally berating myself, I asked the taxi driver to circle it a few times, so I could take some photos. The metal soldier was holding a bayonet-fronted rifle and looked like he meant business, notwithstanding his small stature.

"This is the Clock Tower," said the taxi driver a few minutes later, as we passed the same clock I'd earlier ignored: the one with the battery advertisements.

Bloody hell, I cursed to myself. In my aimless wanderings, I had already passed two of Dar es Salaam's prime sights – and was now paying a taxi driver to show me them again. Wiping my hot brow, I sat back and fumed.

We parked at what seemed to be a ferry terminal of some kind. Lines of people were all heading in the same direction — towards some large gates where the ferries went from. Two women passed our car, carrying large baskets of bananas on their heads. I got out and walked to a wall overlooking the ocean trying to ignore the stares I was getting. The water looked nice and there were a few wooden boats across the other side, but overall, it still wasn't picturesque. But behind me was something impressive — a building that resembled an aircraft control tower. I asked my driver what it was.

"That is the lighthouse."

I took a photo and climbed back in the car. It was time for the Great Kilimanjaro Hunt.

7

"Okay," I said. "All I need now is a couple of bottles of Kilimanjaro lager to take back to the hotel."

"No problem, boss."

The first place we stopped at was a large supermarket. It didn't sell any alcohol whatsoever, and nor did the next shop after that. Undeterred, my amiable driver headed along a main road under the control of a single policewoman. While we sat in the traffic, he looked at me in his rear-view mirror. "Do not worry," he said. "We will find Kilimanjaro. You look like you need it."

The traffic jam was horrendous, but the policewoman in charge looked like a lady not to be trifled with. She had managed to fit her large frame into a white shirt and black skirt. She had pulled her socks up to her knees. With a flick of her baton, she gave our side of the traffic clearance to move forward.

We pulled up at some sort of central area for taxis. My driver wound down his window and spoke to a group of other drivers, obviously asking about the whereabouts of Kilimanjaro Lager outlets. Most of them looked nonplussed, but one man pointed just behind us. Without delay, we parked the car and got out.

"My friend had told me this store will sell the Kilimanjaro," said my driver with a smile. I followed him around a series of turns until we came to a remote outdoor bar. A few men sat at a table drinking. We both went up to the bar.

"Do you sell Kilimanjaro Lager?" I asked the man behind the counter, knowing that they most likely did because of the huge parasols emblazoned with it.

"Yes."

"Great! I'd like to buy two bottles please."

The man nodded and went to the rear of the bar, and there in a deep recess was a tall fridge filled to the brim with Kilimanjaro Lager.

After the driver had dropped me off at my hotel, I paid him a generous fare for the help he'd given me in my quest for beer.

"No problem, boss," he said. "I enjoyed it too."

8

That evening, I sat in the rooftop restaurant of the Holiday Inn and secretly opened one of my bottles. It had been worth the hassle getting them, I thought as I took a gulp. They were about a tenth of the price the hotel was charging. The view from my seat gave me a panorama of the city, and I could see just how high-rise Dar es Salaam was. Construction was going on everywhere, with cranes littering the skyline, a sure fire indication of a city doing well for itself. As the sun went down, I finished my meal and retired to my room.

So my solo trip around East Africa had come to an end, as had my travels around the Dark Continent as a whole. But what an adventure it had been.

Angela and I had haggled our way through the souqs of Morocco, and battled bumsters in The Gambia. We had driven through the lush countryside of Swaziland, and enjoyed a death defying journey up a mountain pass in Lesotho. We'd almost died on the way up to Table Mountain in South Africa, and heard children sing in Senegal. We'd seen the Pyramids in Egypt, and appreciated how much Ethiopia had moved on since the 1980s. We'd also enjoyed the luxury of the Seychelles and Zanzibar, and revelled at endless wildlife of Zambia and Botswana. But throughout all the places we'd visited, I think we had proven that Africa could be a welcoming continent, a place full of surprise, a place full of beauty.

Of course, there will always be the dust, the poverty, the heat and humidity, and there will always be the shysters — that is part of the deal in Africa. But if you dig deep enough, Africa will sparkle inside its rough exterior.

Africa used to be called the Dark Continent. It can't be called that anymore, because it shines with the smiles of its people. They have endured a lot (and are still enduring it) and yet, on the whole, they welcome visitors warmly.

Here's to Africa and its millions of colourful people.

Afterword

Africa is enormous.

The world's second largest continent covers an area of over thirty million square kilometres, which is three times larger than Europe and over four times bigger than Australia. From its most northerly point in Tunisia to its most southerly tip in South Africa, this vast continent stretches for eight thousand kilometres, which would take a passenger jet nine hours to cross. It is further than the distance between London and Las Vegas.

Fifty-five individual nations make up the continent of Africa. The largest is Algeria, which is five thousand times bigger than the smallest, the Seychelles. Africa's newest country is South Sudan, and its oldest is Liberia, their independence granted 164 years apart.

The almost-unknown Equatorial Guinea has the distinction of being Africa's richest country, at least according to data from the World Bank. With its vast oil reserves, money has poured into this tiny nation, a windfall that has unfortunately not reached the pockets of most of its citizens, a state of play common in Africa.

Africa manages to squeeze over a billion people inside its borders. Some of them are the poorest on Earth, living on less than a dollar a day. Indeed, eighteen of the twenty poorest nations on the planet are in Africa. Predictably then, Africa has the highest death rate in the world due to HIV/AIDS. In some countries, a quarter of the population lives and then dies with the disease. This is a shocking statistic. And, because of this, life expectancy in certain parts of Africa is appallingly low. Surviving beyond the age of 45 is considered old age in some countries.

As for tourism, it will be no surprise that Egypt is the most visited country in Africa, closely followed by Morocco and then South Africa. The least-likely tourist destination will not shock anyone: Somalia. But with a newly appointed government and the re-emergence of airline travel to Mogadishu, things may change for this once pirate-infested East African hotspot.

Africa, by its very nature, entices the intrepid, draws in the bold, and appeals to those wanting to sniff adventure and high drama. The lure of a sunset over the River Zambezi, the seduction of witnessing wildlife in the savannah or the simple pleasure of languishing on a beach in the Indian Ocean have captured the imagination of many. Yet, for every tourist who *does* set foot on African soil, there are thousands who do not. To them, the Dark Continent is a dirty place, a land of hidden dangers. It is full of the unknown, bursting with beasts wanting to maim and devour, and packed with people wanting to kill and torment. From carjackings in Johannesburg to rebel attacks in Mali, from revolutions in Libya to violent clashes in the Congo, Africa courts a very dangerous image. But that is also its star attraction. Africa offers a bit of spice!

That said, safety was a primary concern when Angela and I were planning our travels through Africa. We missed out nations with a high risk of kidnap and skipped over countries where soldiers battled along borders. We wanted to enjoy Africa, to revel in its nature and people; we did not want to be snatched or murdered as we did so.

We also wanted to undertake our travels in some degree of comfort. The thought of backpacking our way through Africa did not excite us; neither did the prospect of feeling the wind on our foreheads or observing the spoor of the antelope so we could decide our next point of travel. Staying in a cockroach-infested hostel after dining in a dank restaurant favoured by buzzing mosquitoes was never going to be part of our plan. We would *flashpack* our way around.

I hope this book has given you a flavour of what to expect in Africa; if it has, then I have succeeded.

Finally, I want to thank our good friend, Andrew Billington for proofreading the text. Without his nose for dangling participles and typographical errors, this book would be a poorer version of itself. He even wrote this final paragraph himself.

If you've enjoyed this book about Jason Smart's travels in Africa, then you may also want to read his other books.

The Red Quest
The Balkan Odyssey
Temples, Tuk-Tuks and Fried Fish Lips
Panama City to Rio de Janeiro
Take Your Wings and Fly

Visit **www.theredquest.com** for more information about the author.

Printed in Poland
by Amazon Fulfillment
Poland Sp. z o.o., Wrocław